IDEA-BASED LEARNING

IDEA-BASED LEARNING

A Course Design Process to Promote
Conceptual Understanding

Edmund J. Hansen

1996–2011 15TH ANNIVERSARY

Sty/us
PUBLISHING, LLC.

STERLING, VIRGINIA

Published by Stylus Publishing, LLC
22883 Quicksilver Drive
Sterling, Virginia 20166-2102

Library of Congress Cataloging-in-Publication-Data
Hansen, Edmund, 1952–
    Idea-based learning : a course design process to promote
conceptual understanding / Edmund J. Hansen.—1st ed.
        p.   cm.
    Includes bibliographical references and index.
    ISBN 978-1-57922-613-8 (cloth : alk. paper)
    ISBN 978-1-57922-614-5 (pbk. : alk. paper)
    ISBN 978-1-57922-615-2 (library networkable e-edition)
    ISBN 978-1-57922-616-9 (consumer e-edition)
        1. Education, Higher—Curricula—United States.
2. Curriculum planning—United States.   3. Concept
learning.   I. Title.
LB2361.5.H354   2011
378.1′990973—dc22   2011012805

13-digit ISBN: 978-1-57922-613-8 (cloth)
13-digit ISBN: 978-1-57922-614-5 (paper)
13-digit ISBN: 978-1-57922-615-2 (library networkable
e-edition)
13-digit ISBN: 978-1-57922-616-9 (consumer e-edition)

Printed in the United States of America

All first editions printed on acid free paper
that meets the American National Standards Institute
Z39-48 Standard.

Bulk Purchases

Quantity discounts are available for use in workshops
and for staff development.
Call 1-800-232-0223

First Edition, 2011

10   9   8   7   6   5

CONTENTS

LIST OF FIGURES

ACKNOWLEDGMENTS

M y first forays into course design were inspired by Robert Diamond's 1998 book on the topic and then by Dee Fink's presentations at conferences of the Professional and Organizational Development (POD) Network in Higher Education, and ultimately by his 2003 book *Creating Significant Learning Experiences*. When the time came for me to provide groups of faculty with extensive course design workshops, I eventually discovered the work of Grant Wiggins and Jay McTighe in *Understanding by Design*. Barbara Walvoord and Virginia Johnson Anderson's book *Effective Grading* and on assignment-centered course construction and their colleagues' workshops on course design were another source of inspiration, as were Barbara Tewksbury and Heather Macdonald's online resources for *Designing Effective and Innovative Courses*. Most of the concepts and ideas in this book go back to these sources.

This book owes much to the many faculty members and colleagues at Northeastern Illinois University who worked with me through various versions of my emerging course design model and helped me grow it to the point where it is today. Similarly, my colleagues at POD, who attended my workshops over the last few years, have forced me to both streamline and supplement the way I have structured my ideas. This work would not have been possible without them, nor would it have been possible without the generous grant from the U.S. Department of Education (grant #P031S000096), which allowed my insights to jell for more than six years.

Thank you to ASCD for permission to use examples from Jay McTighe and Grant Wiggins' book, *Understanding by Design: Professional Development Workbook*.

I also want to thank three people who have had a direct influence on the writing and presentation of this work: Deborah Barrett, who copyedited the book; Todd Andrew Irwin, who designed the chapter graphs; and, above all, John von Knorring, president and publisher of Stylus Publishing, whose thoughtful suggestions and unwavering support helped me sharpen my focus and rethink directions on multiple chapters. He and his editorial staff deserve much credit.

Most of all, I want to thank my wife, Siat-Moy Chong, whose patience and encouragement allowed me to pursue this work with its many ups and downs over the years.

Thank you all.

PRACTICAL BENEFITS OF COURSE DESIGN

OVERVIEW

FACULTY STRESSORS IN TEACHING

- Lack of students' intellectual curiosity
- Students' academic underpreparedness
- Fear of antagonizing students
- Time spent on grading papers
- The addition of new teaching roles

BENEFITS FROM IDEA-BASED COURSE DESIGN

- Focus on the big picture gives direction and reduces information overload
- Detailed criteria for quality performance are defined up front
- Ample practice opportunities for key skills are built into the design
- Courses are built around authentic performance tasks
- The emphasis on formative assessment turns the faculty into coaches
- Course activities are structured to overcome students' barriers against critical thinking

IDEA-BASED LEARNING

- Some principles

T his book is a manual for developing college instruction that has a clear purpose, is well-situated in the curriculum, and improves student learning in measurable ways. In addition, it also makes the case that a well-designed, idea-based course is the best insurance for an enjoyable, low-stress teaching and learning experience for faculty and students alike. The process requires faculty to develop a transparent blueprint of their course, one that is focused on several key ideas and meaningful tasks, detailed performance criteria, lots of practice opportunities, and identification of potential learning barriers. In some ways, course design then is akin to preventive medicine. Done carefully, it can help head off many of the ailments faculty endure in their teaching and make life a whole lot easier throughout the semester by reducing or avoiding altogether many of the stressors that faculty tend to experience in the classroom. Let's look at some of those stressors.

Faculty Stressors in Teaching

Lack of Students' Intellectual Curiosity

When faculty talk about what they find most rewarding about their profession, interaction with students usually ranks at the top of their list. After all, student learning is the main reason universities exist, and being able to positively influence others' intellectual growth can be a greatly satisfying experience. It is peculiar, then, that when faculty recount what they find most stressful in their profession, students frequently top that list as well. Of course, this should not come as a surprise because educating students from multiple social and academic backgrounds is a complex business, fraught with many unpredictable challenges and rewards.

Probably one of the most frustrating classroom experiences for faculty is that it seems so difficult to get through to students. The academy wants students to develop an intellectual curiosity and a love of learning that will accompany them throughout their lives. Therefore, we find it hard to stomach that many class sessions are so one-sided, with faculty struggling to get students involved in discussion, only to recognize that most students just don't seem to be that interested in a stimulating exchange of ideas.

Students' Academic Underpreparedness

Closely related to the widespread lack of student curiosity is the frustration with their low levels of academic preparedness. The need for remedial courses is high at all but the most selective universities in the country, with 25% of the freshmen needing developmental courses in one or more disciplines (Gabriel, 2008, p. 1). Most high school students "struggle to understand their textbooks or to communicate what they have learned [. . .]. Seventy percent of eighth graders and 65% of twelfth graders do not read at proficient levels" (Alliance for Excellent Education, Issue Brief, 2007). Some sources claim that only a third of high school graduates nationwide are actually ready for college. (Greene & Winters, 2005). It is small wonder then, that, according to the Higher Education Research Institute's (HERI) 2008 survey of more than 22,000 faculty, 70% of public four-year faculty consider "working with underprepared students" as a source of stress.

Fear of Antagonizing Students

At the same time, a peculiar psychological bond develops between faculty and students. James Lang, recounting his first year on the tenure-track, describes it as follows: "I really want my students to like me. I can think of only one explanation for this strange feeling . . . students are my only indicators . . . capable of telling me whether I am a good professor" (Lang, 2005, p. 71). The work faculty do in the classroom is at once arguably the most important part of their duties and the part for which they receive the least public recognition. Teaching is difficult to evaluate reliably. This is why student evaluations have become by far the most widely used and most influential measure of teaching proficiency. Even if we ignore the institutional relevance of this fact, emotionally the faculty member is dependent on the reactions of his or her students more than anything else. Students are the ones we are trying to impact; their judgment, therefore, is our ultimate reward.

It pains many professors when their role includes not just nurturing their students' intellectual growth, but also having to act as disciplinarians. The latter can take on many forms. There are the disruptive students in class who need to be dealt with, the persistent and sometimes aggressive complaints about grades, the procrastinators who expect extra-credit assignments at the last minute, and so on. Acting "in loco parentis" with young adults who don't show much maturity can be stressful if those same students are called upon to pass judgment on the faculty's teaching performance and possibly their careers.

Time Spent on Grading Papers

Studies of newly hired faculty show that their number-one stressor is the feeling that there simply isn't enough time in the day to do everything that is expected of them (Buckholdt & Miller, 2009; Menges, 1996). Of the 22,000 faculty responding to the HERI survey in 2008, fully 74% said that "lack of personal time" is a source of stress, more than any other classroom-related factor. The most time-consuming component in a faculty's week is class preparation and, within that, the marathon task of grading student papers. What makes the task particularly taxing is the faculty's suspicion that they are working harder on grading than their students did writing those papers. Given their average class preparation time of two to three hours per week, today's students hardly put in the effort to create carefully structured and well-reasoned course papers that would seem to warrant a faculty member's serious consideration and feedback.

The Addition of New Teaching Roles

One final source of stress derives from the changing role of the teaching profession. Until the 1960s, a faculty's role in the classroom was unquestionably that of an information supplier who lectured students on what was important, and students took notes and followed the faculty's lead. That began to change for several reasons: Increased numbers of high school graduates enrolling in college, the doubling of the minority student population, changing demands posed by new information technologies, and the public's call for more accountability in higher education and the outcomes of its products. These changes require teaching strategies that more actively engage students, while at the same time providing more skill-building opportunities for students arriving less prepared for college work. Faculty need to take on new roles by acting more as guides, mentors, technologists, and assessors. All these changes have accelerated in the last two decades and put significant stress on faculty who are torn in many directions.

Benefits From Idea-Based Course Design

Course design that wants to address these stressors will follow principles that are generally aligned with notions of student-centered and outcomes-based learning environments. I am calling it course design for "idea-based learning" to distinguish it from a tradition that puts factual content at the center and results mainly in sequences of loosely related topics and tasks that make up the course syllabus. By contrast, idea-based course design is guided by big conceptual ideas that give structure and unity to a course and even to the curriculum. Following are some of the main features of this type of course design and how they can help with the various stressors that make faculty's class experiences challenging.

Focus on the Big Picture Gives Direction and Reduces Information Overload

A semester is a long time span that involves lots of content knowledge and, taken piece by piece, poses a challenge for students and faculty alike to stay focused on the structure and overall meaning of the course content. Unless big, overarching ideas that hold the content together are provided, the course could appear as one long string of disconnected content bits. What is missing is a larger conceptual framework that makes these pieces meaningful. More of this will be discussed in chapter 3, where learning outcomes are derived from big ideas and enduring understandings, and in chapter 5, which connects learning outcomes with essential questions and guiding concepts.

The often-deplored lack of students' intellectual curiosity may be a direct result of teaching formats that drown students in large pools of information without providing the big picture. Twelve years of schooling have managed to numb many students' curiosity with large quantities of unconnected details. These students will find it difficult to see the big picture in college if they continue to be bombarded by more of the same. The diverse demands of their courses and the various disciplines they encounter in college only perpetuate their sense of alienation with academic content. Unless their courses and curricula provide more coherence and direction for what is important versus what is simply nice to know, college is not likely to encourage their sense of learning for learning's sake.

Detailed Criteria for Quality Performance Are Defined Up Front

In line with emphasizing the big picture, idea-based course design is explicit in its expectations for students' classroom performance. It spells out the criteria for performance on the key tasks in the course with detailed instructions and even work samples for different levels of quality work. Frequently, rubrics are used to describe the characteristics of different performance levels for each criterion provided. This takes the guessing out of grading and empowers students with the ability to assess their own work before it is even handed in. Chapter 7 provides examples on how rubrics can be created and used to both assess and to teach.

Such procedures dramatically reduce potential antagonism between students and faculty, resulting from grades that students perceive as subjective and unfair because the standards have not been articulated or revealed until the work has been handed in. Rubrics also tend to reduce faculty's biggest time killer, grading papers, because faculty comments are referenced to criteria that were established and understood before the assignment was given. They link the grading criteria with the course outcomes and explain to students what the professional standards are in a discipline. Even marginally prepared students can benefit from rubrics, because they point out where students' weaknesses are and what they need to do in order to pass the course.

Ample Practice Opportunities for Key Skills Are Built Into the Design

Traditional course design tends to be content driven and thereby creates time pressures, because there is always more content available than can be covered in a semester. By focusing on less content, idea-based course design makes time for practicing the skills that are deemed important for the students' success in the course. Those skills are broken into their constituent elements (small steps) so that it is easier to see where a student falls short and needs more help. This procedure also addresses the problem of students' academic underpreparedness and integrates help with some of the skills they may be lacking into the structure of the course. Because making time for skill building reduces the content overload of many courses, it directs students' attention to the most significant aspects of the course. Chapter 6 further explains how to provide different types of practice and feedback opportunities to allow students to learn from their mistakes.

Courses Are Built Around Authentic Performance Tasks

Helping students see the big picture is a necessary but insufficient condition for rekindling their intellectual curiosity. Additionally, it takes interesting tasks that challenge students to experience what it means to apply newly gained knowledge in real or simulated contexts. The idea-based approach builds a course around one or more authentic performance tasks that show students the types of problems and issues that an academic discipline addresses. The task requires students to "do" the subject, using judgment and innovation while demonstrating their ability to use a repertoire of knowledge and skills acquired in the course. The task might turn into a semester-long project that is broken into different building blocks for students to work on as the semester progresses. It thereby provides opportunities for practicing a variety of component skills that students need in order to complete the different phases of their project. Chapter 6 outlines the characteristics of an authentic performance task, and chapter 8 further elaborates on assignment-centered instruction and presents different formats of building block designs.

If students are applying their knowledge in a task with unpredictable outcomes for which the students alone are responsible, their attachment to traditional teacher-directed instruction might gradually subside. Producing something that has real-world application is likely to replace any resentment students might otherwise feel toward learner-centered teaching approaches. Identifying and engaging students' own interests in addressing authentic problems is the best way to help them change their dysfunctional expectations toward classroom learning.

The Emphasis on Formative Assessment Turns the Faculty Into Coaches

Engaging students' interests does require faculty to first identify those interests. This illustrates one of the important new roles that faculty have been facing in recent years—the role of assessor. By this, I do not mean the familiar role of grader of student work, but diagnostician of student-learning progress. As students spend time in class practicing new skills and applying knowledge to authentic contexts, faculty gain opportunities to observe and guide student development. Because complex skills have been broken into small steps and students work through these steps by reflecting on their performance and being open to feedback, the faculty's role is changing to that of an assessor and coach, who orchestrates learning environments, listens, and intervenes only when necessary. Faculty have the time to do this, because they are no longer the key providers of knowledge (in the form of lectures), and their feedback is now more appreciated because it is useful for the next steps in the students' work on the authentic performance task. Chapter 6 elaborates on the faculty's coaching role and the importance of student reflection and self-assessment.

Course Activities Are Structured to Overcome Students' Barriers Against Critical Thinking

Diagnosing students' difficulties with particular concepts and skills is a crucial faculty role in idea-based course design. But the literature on student learning has also identified a number of systemic learning barriers, and those barriers are broad threats to the development of critical thinking in general. Those threats fall into several categories, including different phases in the evolution of thought about the learning process, the acquisition of learning-conducive habits of mind, discipline-specific misconceptions on how things work, and logical fallacies in complex reasoning, all described in detail in chapter 4. Course designers need to be aware of these barriers and structure their activities to help students "unlearn" the misconceptions that created the barriers. As they do, faculty will recognize some of the reasons for their students' detrimental behavior, such as their lack of curiosity and their demands for faculty to act as sage on the stage. Only if the course design purposefully addresses these threats can students make progress with their critical thinking skills and climb the ladder of ongoing intellectual development.

Idea-Based Learning

Some Principles

Good course design is based on an understanding of how to best organize student learning in an academic environment. I call my approach "idea-based learning" because it suggests a learning focus that is sorely needed to cope with today's knowledge explosion. Given this proliferation of new knowledge, it is easy to lose sight of what really matters, especially of what our students bring to the classroom and what would enable them to leave that classroom as autonomous learners. Following are the key descriptors of idea-based learning:

- Idea-Based Learning (IBL) is the opposite of Content-Based Learning, which emphasizes the relatively indiscriminate acquisition of knowledge based on content domains or topics.
- IBL emphasizes the big picture so that students don't get lost in myriad details and instead keep a focus on what holds all those details together.
- IBL facilitates conceptual understanding and deep learning.
- IBL recognizes that deep, conceptual understanding is best accomplished by "doing a subject" rather than just hearing or reading about it. Learning by doing requires authentic task contexts that have students perform their assignments under (close to) real-world conditions.
- Instead of merely learning (as in hearing or reading) about issues, students *explore* the issues by asking their own questions, making their

own mistakes, and finding ways to change and improve their initial superficial understanding of the issues.

- In the process, instructors help students discover systematic misconceptions that students held about knowledge, their own habits of mind, the rules of logical reasoning, and fundamental assumptions of their discipline.
- IBL highlights the need for *unlearning* formerly unnoticed misconceptions in the process of advancing to more sophisticated levels of understanding. Students' reflective self-assessment is a crucial part of their education.
- IBL builds student competencies not around content, but around the application of concepts in the context of authentic performance tasks that help students explore the issues that matter most for solving problems.

These learning theoretical ideas are not entirely new, of course. Many of them have been around since the times of John Dewey. In more recent years, they have been expressed by educators and curriculum designers such as Lynn Erickson, Barbara Walvoord, and Grant Wiggins and his colleague Jay McTighe. I especially owe a large debt to the latter for the insights they have laid out in *Understanding by Design* (Wiggins & McTighe, 2005) as well as in *Educative Assessment* (Wiggins, 1998). Those insights are reflected throughout the chapters of this book and have enabled me to construct my own framework for how to build a college course step-by-step.

THE BACKWARD COURSE DESIGN MODEL

1.
IDENTIFY DESIRED RESULTS

a. Big Ideas
b. Enduring Understandings
c. Learning Outcomes
d. Student Background

2.
DETERMINE ACCEPTABLE EVIDENCE

a. Main Assessment Tasks
b. Rubrics
c. Competencies
d. Practice Opportunities

3.
PLAN MAIN LEARNING EXPERIENCES

a. Authentic Performance Tasks
b. Building Blocks
c. Practice Activities Suitable for Competencies

4.
SEQUENCE COURSE CONTENT AROUND ACTIVITIES

a. Developmental Sequences of Learning Modules
b. Combination of Learning Modules With Practice Activites
c. Packaging of Course Content With Activites

Note: Chapter Graphs were created by Todd Andrew Irwin

2

BACKWARD DESIGN

OVERVIEW

T**RADITIONAL COURSE DESIGN**

- How do faculty spend their time when designing a course?
- Which course design approaches have been documented by research?
- The flowchart of traditional course design
- How are course goals/outcomes established?

C**RITIQUE OF THE TRADITIONAL DESIGN**

- Why faculty might not believe in course design
- Where is the student in traditional course design?
- How does the "logic of the content" differ from the "logic of learning the content"?

T**HE BACKWARD DESIGN MODEL**

- What is curricular alignment?

T**HE IMPORTANCE OF COURSE DESIGN**

- How course and curriculum development fit together

Traditional Course Design

How Do Faculty Spend Their Time When Designing a Course?

I asked a few of the faculty groups that went through my workshops how they spend their time planning for a course. This was an unscientific survey of only 13 people, more of a warm-up exercise than a data collection. Nevertheless, the results were telling. Of the four options they could choose, seven faculty spent most of their time selecting their instructional strategies, while only two each focused on defining their learning outcomes, planning to assess student learning, or selecting the main course concepts.

The results were not unexpected because the outcomes-based assessment movement is still fairly young in higher education. Faculty tend to hear about it mainly when their program or their campus is preparing for reaccreditation and the self-study guidelines require them to present learning outcomes and evidence of assessment of these outcomes. Although most professional educators admit that outcomes-based assessment represents a paradigm shift in how we approach course and curriculum design, little training is offered to help faculty understand the new paradigm and, frankly, who would want to learn new ways of doing things when no help is offered for trying?

Which Course Design Approaches Have Been Documented by Research?

Innovators are not doing too well in championing changes when they don't really know the current ways in which faculty do their work. There is regretfully little research on how exactly faculty go about designing their courses. Probably the most thorough investigation done in recent years is a qualitative study of faculty at Widener University in Chester, Pennsylvania. The faculty development director at the institution, Donna Harp Ziegenfuss (2007a, 2007b), looked at how 23 faculty members designed their courses, and she managed to summarize their approaches into five different categories:

1. Needs-focused course design: Faculty looked at factors related to their student population. Key student characteristics included students' prior experiences, level of students' place in the program, majors vs. non-majors, and so on.

2. Outcomes-based course design: Faculty started with the intended student learning outcomes for the course and then "aligned" all other components of the course with the achievement of those outcomes.

3. Course design within a structure or framework: Faculty fit their course into a structure that either they themselves defined (e.g., a list of topics to follow) or that was imposed externally (e.g., by departmental demands for use of certain textbooks or a list of special topics or program outcomes).

4. Course design based on a process or sequence driven: Faculty designed a plan of action for how to guide students through the learning experience in a way that allowed for easier understanding and the making of meaningful connections.

5. Course design as a part of a bigger picture: Faculty made connections between their course and the bigger picture of the program, department, or institution, and goals were aligned across these different levels. (Ziegenfuss, 2007a)

Ziegenfuss notes that these approaches were not mutually exclusive, and that "faculty used several of the five course design categories . . . simultaneously . . . to shape their own personal approach to course design" (POD handout, p. 2). Given these descriptions, one might say that format #3 and possibly format #1 are most closely related to what I call the "traditional" approach, but it is obvious that even an in-depth study of 23 faculty on one campus cannot claim to be representative of thousands of faculty at hundreds of different institutions of higher education.

Therefore, as I begin this chapter by contrasting "the traditional" with a new format, I can hardly claim a solid research base for this distinction. It is likely that these are merely two ends of a spectrum, across which a large variety of approaches are practiced. I base my description of the traditional format on inferences from working with dozens of faculty on course design, discussing new course proposals on curriculum-review committees, and looking through hundreds of syllabi that do not indicate a conceptual framework, although, admittedly, syllabi tend to be a poor representation of the actual structure of a course.

The Flowchart of Traditional Course Design

With this caveat, I present a simplified flowchart showing how this prototypically "traditional" course design format might look (see figure 2.1). (For a description of the traditional with two newer frameworks that compares assessment practices, see Stiehl & Lewchuk, 2002, p. 17.) The readers have to judge how closely my description matches their own experiences.

The most outstanding characteristic of this design is that it is content driven. Faculty are experts in their fields and like to talk about courses they teach in terms of the content they cover. Their love for their disciplines easily takes over the planning of their courses. This approach emphasizes the knowledge base of the discipline and is filtered through any preferences the instructor has regarding his or her own specialization in the field or research paradigm. To speed up the process, textbooks come in handy, especially in the case of planning lower-level courses. If a textbook is used as the course blueprint, the next decision is typically connected with the time constraints that are inherent in any course. Textbooks tend to have too many chapters, therefore, deciding what to cut is important in adjusting coverage to a manageable rate. Instructors base their decisions on their personal preferences in the discipline, their knowledge of student interest and ability, and their desire to personalize the course material by adding supplemental text materials to the content in the textbook. Most instructors add this "personal touch" to distinguish their course from others using the same book. It also helps make the course more interesting, because textbooks tend to follow the same uninspired format that students have known since the early days of their schooling.

Besides supplementing the textbook with other readings, instructors' best options for putting their own stamp on the course are the course assignments. Here creativity might be called for when coming up with a task, or a set of tasks, that inspires students to take an active role in their learning, if not in the course itself. Students might be asked to apply key course content to a topic of their choosing, express their reflections in a journal, or prepare an oral presentation that further extends the scope of the course content. Other considerations might also enter the instructor's planning at this point, such as, "How can I distinguish the outstanding student from the rest?" "What can I do to break up too much continued lecturing?" "How can I make sure that students keep up with the readings and are able and willing to participate in class discussions?" This could ultimately lead to the question: "What are the students' roles in the class, and how can they be worked into the design of course assignments?" If the faculty member is focused on covering the course content, defining an active-student role in the class can become challenging.

FIGURE 2.1
The Traditional Course Design Model

1. Start with course content:

a) Especially at the lower course levels, using the chapters of a textbook provides a convenient guide for mapping out the content that needs to be covered.

b) Because most textbooks contain too much material, decide which chapters to drop.

c) Are there other readings that should supplement the textbook?

2. Plan what students need to do:

a) Now that the instructor knows what to cover, the students' main role(s) in the course needs to be determined. The minimum requirement is that they take some tests and complete one or more assignments.

b) Assignments identify how the students line up on a scale from "A" to "F." They also enforce student participation in the course.

3. Decide how to assign grades:

a) Grading procedures are developed that allow the instructor to use his/her professional judgment while minimizing students' suspicion of grader-subjectivity.

b) Grading on the curve is often used to correct instructor misjudgment of student capabilities and guarantee a "balanced" representation of student learning.

4. Deduct what students should gain from your instruction:

a) The main goal is that students understand the content you teach. Here is how that content could be summarized into a few key points (called "objectives").

b) If students typically lack in an important skill domain (such as writing), turn improvement in this skill into another course objective.

c) If students typically lack in an important professional attitude (such as "an appreciation for . . ."), turn development of this attitude into another course objective.

1. Create or adapt course content	a. Select textbook/ readings b. Select chapters for coverage c. Consider additional readings
2. Plan assignments and test	a. Create assignments that separate good from poor students b. Create small assignments to maintain student participation
3. Determine grading procedures	a. Grade according to professional judgment b. Consider grading on the curve
4. Translate course content into instructor objectives	a. Turn key topics of the course into objectives b. Consider key course skills as course objectives c. Consider development of professional attitude as objective

Student assessment is closely linked with class assignments. The old standby is still "two tests and a paper." Too often the process of developing an assessment plan for a course consists largely of evenly spreading out tests and other graded activities across the semester and assigning the appropriate weight to each. However, additional agendas typically hide behind grading scales. As experts in their fields, faculty tend to be suspicious of quantifying their judgment of the quality of student performance. When asked to do so, they often resort to assigning tasks that lend themselves to quantifying, such as multiple-choice tests of factual knowledge. Because some open-ended tasks are usually included in the grading mix, holistic grading of the students' conceptual understanding and critical thinking tends to cause controversy. Contentious students frequently question their instructors' judgment. As a result, grading on the curve becomes a temptation that seems to remedy both student complaints and faculty discomfort with putting a quantitative value on students' higher-order thinking ability. A third agenda hiding behind student assessment emerges when grading turns into a tool for reward and punishment, for achieving student compliance. Spreading out assignments or tests with significant point values across the semester serves to reduce procrastination among students who only study when something is at stake.

How Are Course Goals/Outcomes Established?

Coming up with course objectives (or learning outcomes, as they are called nowadays) is often left until the end. Objectives tend to be a summary of the main things an instructor wants to cover in a course, thereby representing the highlights of the most important course content. Besides content, other course purposes might be added as objectives, such as the development of good writing skills, an appreciation of the contributions of the discipline, or an overall love for lifelong learning. However, because these are rather lofty goals, they are usually phrased in broad terms, suggesting the instructor's hopes that the course will contribute to students' improvement in these areas, even though no particular means for assessing them are mentioned.

Critique of the Traditional Design

Why Faculty Might Not Believe in Course Design

One of the biggest problems with traditional course design is the barely hidden doubt in the need for course design at all. Stigler and Hiebert (1997) claim: "Americans hold the notion that good teaching comes through artful and spontaneous interactions with students during lessons. . . . Such views minimize the importance of planning increasingly effective lessons . . ." (p. 20). If course design is mainly a matter of laying out the content for the students, and faculty are the experts in that content, then one expert's design/layout is probably as valid as another's, and the distinguishing factor is how the content is delivered in the classroom. Clearly, some teachers are better than others at establishing rapport with their students and engaging them in discussion of the material. Under those circumstances, design takes a backseat to performance and "spontaneous interactions" in the classroom.

Where Is the Student in Traditional Course Design?

The traditional student role is that of recipient of instructor-explained course content; students are the faculty audience. They are expected to make a good-faith effort to understand the faculty's lectures, raise questions when they don't understand, and engage in dialogue when faculty decide to interrupt their lecture through a question-and-answer activity. In addition, students demonstrate their understanding of faculty-conveyed content by writing a term paper or summarizing their paper in a short presentation of their own. Overall, there is little effort by the instructor to use the classroom as a laboratory to diagnose the students' strengths and weaknesses and to tailor the instruction to those learner needs.

How Does the "Logic of the Content" Differ From the "Logic of Learning the Content"?

Wiggins and McTighe (2005) distinguish the "logic of the content itself" from the "logic of learning (or performing with) content" (p. 292). Traditional course design uses the logic of the content as the guide for building a course. That logic typically has a hierarchical structure, where one starts with basic concepts and gradually refines them to become more complex and sophisticated. Alternatively, the instructor might follow a chronological approach, starting with what came earlier (say, in the history of the discipline) and continuing with insights developed more recently. Whatever structure the content takes, it's an ongoing progression designed to avoid redundancy and repetition.

By comparison, the logic of learning the content is quite different, because it considers the students and their need to go back and forth between the details and the big picture. Redundancy and repetition, whole-part-whole activities, are crucial to help students make connections and develop a "conceptual schema for building deep understanding over time" (Erickson, 2002, p. 8). Wiggins and McTighe (2005) use the example of computer-assisted tutorials. Here the flow of learning is determined by students acquiring limited chunks of content by immediately applying them to a task before moving on to other, increasingly complicated content.

In a course that merely follows the logic of the content, objectives are established so that students will follow a prescribed path to the "truths" of the discipline. Deviations from that path are discouraged; mistakes must be avoided. As a result, the acquired knowledge remains abstract and inert, and students do not make that knowledge their own. Learning is seen as a uniform process of acquiring predetermined bits of knowledge that instructors "feed" their students. On the other hand, the logic of learning the content emphasizes the learner's sense-making of the content. That process is nonlinear, often riddled with detours and mistakes, and guided by questions to which students need to find their own answers. Students experiment with the content rather than passively absorb it. This generates depth of understanding and eventually the opportunity to move beyond the knowledge as it currently exists.

The logic of learning the content in depth is the foundation for idea-based learning. In the 1970s, researchers Ference Marton, Roger Saljo, Noel Entwistle, and Paul Ramsden started their studies on how students approached learning as they moved through school. They discovered a similar pattern in the logic behind students' learning approaches, which they called "deep learning" versus "surface learning." The latter was satisfied with receiving information passively and memorizing unconnected facts, whereas the former actively tried to relate parts of the subject matter to each other and to the real world. Depth resulted from grasping underlying ideas that allowed students to actively reinterpret knowledge and understand reality in a different way (see Saljo, 1979). This would lead to what Dee Fink calls "significant learning." Such learning "requires that there be some kind of lasting change that is important in terms of the learner's life" (2003, p. 30). Unfortunately, some studies suggest "that students progressively drop the deep approach to learning as they move through high school and college. It appears that in many ways, traditional teaching pushes students toward superficial levels of engagement with material" (Rhem, 1995). To achieve deep/significant learning, instructors need to organize their courses in ways that are more exploratory and focused on the big picture.

The Backward Design Model

In 1949, Ralph Tyler published what was to become the most influential model in course and curriculum design to date. Though clearly influenced by behaviorism and ideas of technical job analysis (or "task analysis"), Tyler's basic idea of starting with the intended end state in the learning process and working one's way backward to determine what needs to happen to reach that state is still powerful. Tyler summarized his "backward" approach into four key questions:

1. What educational purposes should the [course or curriculum] seek to attain?
2. How can learning experiences be selected that are likely to be useful in attaining these objectives?
3. How can learning experiences be organized for effective instruction?
4. How can the effectiveness of learning experiences be evaluated?

What Is Curricular Alignment?

The important idea here is that once learning outcomes ("educational purposes") have been carefully selected, everything that happens in a course (or ultimately in a whole curriculum) must be designed toward making the achievement of these outcomes possible. This alignment of learning outcomes with assessment procedures and well-organized learning experiences makes systematic course design possible. Although course content remains important, it no longer provides the structure around which courses and curricula are created. The design process focuses on the accomplishment of student insights and skills that require thoughtful orchestration of learning experiences tailor-made to help in the students' struggle for conceptual understanding.

Post-Tyler developments on student-centered learning have shifted the emphasis even more onto the learners and their experiential backgrounds and motivational dispositions. They, together with the course content, determine what the appropriate learning outcomes are for a given course. Outcomes are not simply acquired bodies of knowledge, but the ability to do something with that knowledge that has meaning for the student. This requires learning experiences with many practice opportunities, in which students can make mistakes and discover what's important as they integrate course content into their own cognitive schemas. Figure 2.2 illustrates how alignment of the four or five main design components is established.

FIGURE 2.2
Curricular Alignment

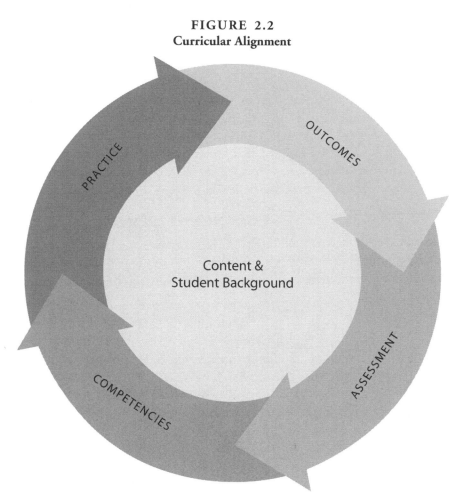

Not surprisingly, this design process is circular in nature; each element influences the next one. Although the process starts with selection of the learning outcomes, they might have to be adjusted once the other components have been considered. The graph should be read as follows:

1. Looking at the current state of the discipline, the course level, and the students' background, define appropriate *learning outcomes* for your course.

2. To *assess* whether your learning outcomes are achieved, design meaningful performance tasks that allow you to judge students' understanding of the course content.

3. To help students do well on these performance tasks, create effective *learning experiences* that provide practice opportunities of required competencies.

4. To find appropriate practice opportunities, emphasize the *content* that best exemplifies your learning outcomes.

Alignment of learning outcomes with student assessment and classroom-learning experiences is the crucial characteristic of this course design approach. However, creating alignment is not an easy thing to do, no matter how logical it might sound. Future chapters on assessment and course content will demonstrate how alignment can be accomplished. For now, a graphic of the step-by-step procedure that represents the backward design model will suffice (see figure 2.3).

The Importance of Course Design

I mentioned earlier the doubts that faculty might have about the need for systematic course design and how these doubts are based on the notion that "good teaching comes through artful and spontaneous interactions with students during lessons" (Stigler & Hiebert, 1997, p. 16). Curriculum designers provide a different viewpoint. They claim that the traditional course design, which merely follows "the logic of the content" and emphasizes teaching performance over student learning, has not served us well. Lynn Erickson states:

> The traditional design of a curriculum emphasizes the lower cognitive levels, centering around topics and related facts. This curriculum design, which has been driving teaching and learning in our country for more than 100 years, must be addressed if we are ever going to raise educational standards. It does little good to engage students with performance if our curriculum design aims the display of understanding no higher than the topic. (2002, pp. 4–5)

Facts and topics engage only the lowest levels of student cognition, with concepts, principles, and theories occupying the highest levels. As long as

FIGURE 2.3
The Backward Course Design Model (Annotated)

1. Identify desired results	**1. Determine what students should get out of this course:**
a. Big Ideas b. Enduring Understandings c. Learning Outcomes d. Student Background	a) Brainstorm your discipline's most relevant big ideas. b) Identify which enduring understandings can be derived from these big ideas. c) Create a manageable number of learning outcomes that relate to these enduring understandings. d) Anticipate areas in which students are likely to struggle with the course content.
2. Determine acceptable evidence	**2. Determine how to assess whether students have achieved the learning outcomes:**
a. Main Assessment Tasks b. Rubrics c. Needed Abilities d. Practice Opportunities	a) Create the main assessment tasks as "authentic performance tasks." b) Create rubrics for those tasks with a few key criteria. c) Define a set of abilities that are required for students to perform well on each criterion. d) Decide on specific practice opportunities to help students acquire those abilities.
3. Plan main learning experiences	**3. Design learning experiences around these assessment tasks:**
a. Authentic Performance Tasks b. Building Blocks c. Practice Activities Suitable for Needed Abilities	a) Take each authentic performance task as the basis on which to organize the learning experiences of the course. b) Break big tasks and assignments into smaller building blocks ("learning modules"). c) Attach the appropriate practice activities to each building block.
4. Sequence course content around activities	**4. Create a developmental sequence for the learning experiences throughout the semester and organize course content around them:**
a. Developmental Sequences of Learning Modules b. Combination of Learning Modules With Practice Activities c. Packaging of Course Content With Activities	a) Spread the building blocks of your main assignments strategically over the whole course. b) Outline the sequence of practice activities within each building block. c) Organize your course content around these assignments and activities.

the focus of instruction is concentrated on the content, the decision on what to address in a course has little guidance other than the personal preferences of the instructor or the textbook author. Whereas breadth of knowledge has its benefits, the more important task of effective teaching is the selection of what has the best chances for increasing students' conceptual understanding of the modes of thinking in the field. Figure 2.4 illustrates the decisions that instructional planning has to make:

FIGURE 2.4
Three Levels of Importance for Course Content

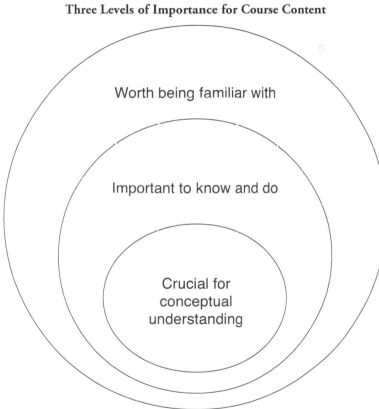

(Adapted from Wiggins & McTighe, 2005, p. 71)

Without a clear rationale for how to choose learning outcomes based on student needs and intellectual readiness, instructors might wander with little guidance across all three circles/levels of course content. Every discipline has an almost endless wealth of information, and it is easy to get bogged down by what is "worth being familiar with" and hardly ever progress toward what is "crucial for conceptual understanding." The likelihood of this happening is particularly high because interesting facts and topics provide easy material for "objective" testing and uncontroversial student grading.

Outcomes-based course design avoids this pitfall. The instructor has a clear roadmap for what is important and what is merely interesting in a course. But it isn't simply a matter of selecting more-relevant over less-relevant material. If the focus is on learning outcomes, the instructional process concentrates on student learning rather than faculty performance. In the outcomes-based curriculum, the instructor's role is to orchestrate learning rather than to deliver instruction. In order to accomplish this, instructors need to be focused on understanding and facilitating students' evolving comprehension processes. That's what it means to follow the logic of *learning* the content.

Beyond the individual classroom level, there are other important consequences for effective, outcomes-based course design. The reality of teaching in an academic program oftentimes consists of multiple faculty and part-time instructors teaching multiple sections of the same course to satisfy student demand, especially at the undergraduate level. I suspect that it is more the rule than the exception that multiple instructors for different sections of the same course vary dramatically in what they teach in each of those sections. Currently, the only document that represents what happens in a course is the course syllabus. It is not uncommon for course syllabi for different sections of the same course to list different learning outcomes, different assessment procedures, different textbooks, and even different content altogether. Current college teaching seems to lack an effective means for representing what should be the blueprint of a given course. Even where faculty are cognizant of each other's syllabi, these syllabi say very little about the type of learning a given course is trying to accomplish. Most of what can be gleaned from a typical syllabus is content in terms of topics and reading assignments, followed by course policies and grading procedures. Under those circumstances, it is difficult to create a sense of curricular cohesion and accountability for what happens from course section to course section. Other than a vague resemblance of course topics, there is oftentimes no tool for indicating the commonalities across those sections.

How Course and Curriculum Development Fit Together

What is true for sections of the same course applies even more to courses within a whole curriculum. They, too, tend to be carved up by content domains in the field, so that topics and subfields become the only means of building the structure of a curriculum. Student learning outcomes rarely provide the guideposts for defining and connecting different courses that share a program context. Having a curriculum means more than accumulating a body of knowledge; it assumes the development of skills and insights that cut across individual courses. These skills and insights are introduced in some courses, elaborated on in others, and used creatively in yet a third set of courses. Without following a plan for when and where all this happens, achieving proficiency is largely left to chance. It is, therefore, not surprising that systematic program assessment tends to be an almost impossible task when outcomes are poorly defined and even more poorly coordinated across courses.

Problems escalate when connections are required across fields. Interdisciplinarity is rapidly becoming a standard for a more student-centered, authentic learning environment. General education has always had the potential, if not the mandate, for looking beyond the boundaries of individual disciplines. And yet, as long as discipline-internal curricula show little purposeful connectivity across individual courses, connections across disciplines will remain even more tenuous. The next chapter will show how "backward course design" facilitates drawing those conceptual links across courses and disciplines that make curricula and interdisciplinary teaching meaningful.

FROM BIG IDEAS TO LEARNING OUTCOMES

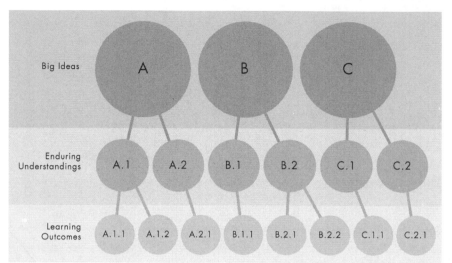

3

LEARNING OUTCOMES

OVERVIEW

PROBLEMS WITH (CONCEPTUALIZING) LEARNING OUTCOMES

- Why formulate goals at all?
- A history of changing terminology

IDENTIFYING BIG IDEAS

- First, look at the curriculum!
- How to establish priorities

DERIVING ENDURING UNDERSTANDINGS

- Connecting big ideas with student horizons
- Which understandings are enduring?

DETERMINING LEARNING OUTCOMES

- How general and how specific should they be?
- Examples from specific courses
- Linking them with different "facets of understanding"

Problems With (Conceptualizing) Learning Outcomes

Why Formulate Goals at All?

The opening paragraphs of many course syllabi tend to contain a set of good intentions that advertise why students should enroll in this course. The goals provided tend to be general, emphasizing the importance of the course content. They are followed by other, more mundane descriptions of course procedures and weekly topics that have no visible connection with the opening goals. Consequently, students pay little attention and would be hard-pressed to recall any course goals when asked to do so at any time in the semester.

A History of Changing Terminology

This practice is not that surprising. After all, instructional designers, state curriculum committees, and regional accreditation bodies have done their best over the years to confuse faculty with ever-changing terminology—from goals to objectives, competencies, behavioral objectives, and learning outcomes—that have practitioners wondering what purpose they actually serve. Linda Suskie (2004) addresses the confusing terminology, pointing out the often interchangeable use of goals and outcomes. "Learning outcomes, also referred to as learning goals, are the knowledge, skills, attitudes, and habits of mind that students take with them from a learning experience" (p. 75). According to Suskie, a goal "explains why we do what we do" rather than merely describing what tasks students are asked to perform. So instead of saying, "students will write a term paper," the goal is for students "to become effective writers" (p. 74).

Curriculum specialists noticed that such goals were too broad to guide instruction in a particular course, so they devised the term *behavioral objectives* to focus on more detailed aspects of a goal. Behavioral objectives provided more specificity by stating learning goals, using concrete *action words/verbs* that defined what students were able to do after learning the material (Suskie, 2004). This had the added bonus of the behavioral goal virtually dictating how its accomplishment was to be assessed. For example:

Broad Goal: Students understand the biology of human life.

Behavioral Objective: Students are able to explain why each planet except Earth cannot support human life.

Assessment: Students write a short explanation of why each planet except Earth cannot support human life. (p. 77)

Unfortunately, the narrow focus of behavioral objectives wi
words suggesting small performance tasks does not always capture enough
of what we want students to learn about a certain subject matter. If the goal
is to truly "understand" something, then a single action might not sufficiently establish student learning; therefore, it might take a series of behavioral objectives to adequately describe one learning goal. This shortcoming
of behavioral objectives led to the more recent shift toward "learning outcomes," which move away from the overly concrete actions demanded of
students in favor of abilities students gain and maintain for the rest of their
lives, as explained in this chapter.

In addition to the confusion about terminology, there is a long-standing
distrust among faculty about planning the instructional process in great
detail. True to the notion of teaching as art, faculty might be skeptical of a
small set of goals that determines all the assignments, assessments, and learning activities in the course. Instead, teaching is seen as the instructor's ability
to spontaneously react to a given classroom situation, and "too much" planning might jeopardize such spontaneity. From that viewpoint, a vaguely
defined assignment might be seen as a virtue because it removes overly rigid
restrictions and allows students to interpret the task in their own way, thus
presumably fostering student creativity.

So once again, why should we formulate goals at all? Because goals and
learning outcomes are important for positioning a single course within the
bigger picture of the curriculum (see chapter 2). Part of the problem with
ill-defined and largely overlooked course outcomes is the lack of planning
for coherent curricula in higher education. Curricula tend to be built more
around the content of subfields in the discipline than around interconnec-
tions, skill domains, and modes of thinking. Academic departments are
rarely in the habit of having ongoing dialogues about curriculum matters,
especially as to how the various courses in the program connect with each
other. To top things off, the practice of hiring new instructors with little
orientation to the fit of their courses with those taught by other faculty adds
to curricular disjuncture. As long as there is lack of structure and coherence,
individual courses have to fend for themselves in defining purpose and goals.
Those goals or learning outcomes will seem random, without foundation,
and with little function for the activities of the classroom.

Idea-based learning and course design require clear definition of purpose. Both instructor and students need to be aware of where a course is
headed, what its main goals are, and why these goals were chosen. That
applies not only to individual courses, but also to how courses are situated

within the curriculum. The important ideas of a given discipline are not confined to a specific course but connect and integrate courses with each other and with other disciplines.

Identifying Big Ideas

First, Look at the Curriculum!

The appropriate point to start identifying learning outcomes for a course is, therefore, the program's curriculum and its broad goals. What should students be taking away from a program after they have gone through all its courses? Department faculty need to agree on a set of emphases for each course in order to function as a building block within the overall curriculum. The course may focus on only one or two of the curriculum goals, but those few goals must guide the learning outcomes that the course pursues (see figure 3.1).

However, even programs with well-developed curricula present any given course with a range of choices as a suitable set of learning outcomes. Where do faculty find guidance for which outcomes to choose? Defining good learning outcomes for a course is indeed a difficult task. First of all, one has to find the right scope. Course outcomes are located between program goals and daily lesson outcomes; they are not as broad as the former and not as narrow as the latter. Secondly, given any field and any course topic within a discipline, almost endless options exist for selecting learning outcomes. And finally, learning outcomes are not confined to knowledge. In fact, knowledge is usually embedded in a good learning outcome that might focus on a skill or an attitude, such as developing a habit for skeptical questioning of assumptions. What is needed is a procedure for devising a rationale that makes the identification of good learning outcomes less random. The next paragraphs will outline a three-step funnel process that provides such rationales. Here I am following the first two steps in the conceptual framework by Wiggins and McTighe (McTighe & Wiggins, 2004; Wiggins & McTighe, 2005) and their richly documented notions of "big ideas" and "enduring understandings" that can be extended and used in the purposeful selection of learning outcomes.

The challenge the authors are responding to with their approach to course design is the fact that "we can never have enough time" (Wiggins & McTighe, 2005, p. 44). Students need to learn far more than we can teach them, and they have to do most of this learning on their own. Therefore,

FIGURE 3.1

Example of Alignment Between Course and Program Goals

Psychology 624: Theories of Motivation

Big Ideas	Enduring Understandings	Learning Outcomes	APA Program Outcomes	APA Program Goals
Motivators of behavior	Behavior is influenced by *external* incentives and *internal* needs.	Students become aware of previously *unnoticed reasons* for the degree of their own intellectual *curiosity*, desire to *achieve*, and their *self-concept*.	OBJ. 9.2: Apply psychological principles to promote personal development, e.g., self-assess performance quality accurately.	GOAL 9: Personal Development: Develop insight into their own and others' behavior and mental processes and apply effective strategies for self-management and self-improvement.
	Motivation involves the interaction of *emotion* and *cognition*.	Explain how cognitive mechanisms can help people overcome motivational tendencies such as *anger* and *defeatism*.	OBJ. 9.2: Apply psychological principles to promote personal development, e.g., demonstrate self-regulation in setting and achieving goals.	GOAL 9 (s.a.)

FIGURE 3.1 (Continued)

Big Ideas	Enduring Understandings	Learning Outcomes	APA Program Outcomes	APA Program Goals
Individual differences	Motivation varies in *intensity* and *type*.	Recognize people's reasons for *seeking or avoiding* certain behaviors or experiences.	OBJ. 1.3: Use the concepts, language, and major theories of the discipline to account for psychological phenomena.	GOAL 1: Knowledge Base: Demonstrate familiarity with the major concepts, theoretical perspectives, empirical findings, and historical trends in psychology.
	Motivation varies *across people from different cultural backgrounds.*	Interpret *individual differences* within cultural contexts.	OBJ. 8.3: Explain how individual differences influence beliefs, values, and interactions with others and vice versa.	GOAL 8: Sociocultural and International Awareness: Recognize, understand, and respect the complexity of sociocultural and international diversity.
Psychological theorizing	Research on motivation has moved from grand to mini-theories.	Identify practical implications of *different motivation-theoretical approaches.*	OBJ. 2.3: Evaluate the appropriateness of conclusions derived from psychological research.	GOAL 2: Research Methods: Understand and apply basic research methods in psychology, including research design, data analysis, and interpretation.
	Self-reports (a basis for some motivation theories) are *susceptible to errors.*	Learn to reflect on causes for own behavior while being critical of possible shortcomings of such *introspection.*	OBJ. 2.6: Generalize research conclusions appropriately based on the parameters of particular research methods.	GOAL 2 (s.a.)

Note: In this case, curriculum goals and outcomes were taken from an outline suggested by the American Psychological Association.

the task for teachers is to prepare students to be able to transfer important concepts and principles from our classrooms to contexts outside those classrooms. This is a tall order, and we know from research (Haskell, 2000; Mestre, 2005) that knowledge transfer is one of the hardest (and least successful) tasks of teaching. How do we decide what is most important to study and what will best serve as a foundation for further independent learning?

This is where the notion of big ideas comes in. *Big ideas* is a decidedly nontechnical term that means just what it says: "The big ideas connect the dots for the learner by establishing learning priorities. . . . they serve as 'conceptual Velcro'—they help the facts and skills stick together and stick in our minds!" (Wiggins & McTighe, 2005, p. 66).

Some big ideas are major theories in a given discipline, such as the theory of evolution in biology or the plate-tectonics model in geology. Those examples demonstrate one of the key aspects of the nature of big ideas, namely, that they are "the hard-won results of inquiry" (Wiggins & McTighe, 2005, p. 67). They emerged at a certain point in the history of the discipline and sometimes revolutionized the thinking in that discipline.

But not all big ideas are quite that conspicuous. Some simply look like core concepts, for example, "social structures" in sociology, "language families" in linguistics, "fundamental building blocks" in biology, or "correlation" in statistics. (For more examples, see figure 3.2.) Even though nowadays they might seem like simple "terminology" that has found its way into everyday discourse, all these concepts were once scientific revelations that have since become standard parts of the academic vocabulary. Nevertheless, whole scientific domains would look different if those concepts were missing.

Big ideas are a result of how scientists theorize about the subject of their discipline. They might be expressed as concepts, but they are more than just basic terms. For example, *statistical error* is a big idea, but *error* is just a term; *experimental method* is a big idea, *experiment* is a term; *natural selection* (big idea) vs. *selection* (term); *negative space* (big idea in art) vs. *space* (term). Big ideas are not necessarily "big" in the sense of covering the most territory in their disciplines. They are essential to their disciplines but might cover more or less ground. The important aspect is that they represent crucial insights and, therefore, require students to uncover for themselves what makes them so valuable.

All this might sound as though big ideas only relate to the content of a discipline, but that is not the case. Courses teach not only content but also

FIGURE 3.2
Different Types of Big Ideas

Disciplinary Content Ideas
(largely specific to individual disciplines)

PSYCHOLOGY:
  Causes of human behavior
  Individual differences
  Free will vs. determinism
  Mind-body interaction
  Interaction of heredity and environment
  Cross-cultural dis-/continuities

SOCIOLOGY:
  Social structures
  Social inequality
  Social institutions
  Culture (and subcultures)
  Ideology
  Social construction

LINGUISTICS:
  (Animal vs. human) communication
  Regional and social dialects
  First language acquisition
  Language origins
  Sociolinguistics
  Syntax
  Language families

BIOLOGY:
  Theory of evolution
  Interdependent ecosystems
  Cell communication networks
  Life (vs. inanimate)
  Metabolic cycles
  Fundamental building blocks
  Thermodynamics

GEOLOGY:
  Plate-tectonics model
  Relativity of time and space
  Earth's dynamic equilibrium system
  Non-/renewable supplies of energy
  Natural hazards
  Fluid spheres within the Earth's system

STATISTICS:
  Central Tendency
  Sampling
  Correlation
  Degrees of confidence
  Prediction

Skills Ideas
(most of them relevant for many disciplines)
• Theorizing: forming hypotheses
• Nonjudgmental observation
• Metacognitive awareness (Self-assessment)
• Applying the scientific method
• Developing career goals
• Seeking out diverse perspectives
• Effective collaboration
• Taking a leadership role
• Conflict resolution/problem solving
• Persuasive writing

Attitudes and Value Ideas
(applicable across disciplines)
• Attitude of critical thinking
• Sociocultural awareness
• Development of professional values
• Importance of lifelong learning
• Commitment to pursuit of knowledge and truth
• Tolerance for ambiguity
• Tolerance of others' views
• Social accountability

Abstract Concept Ideas
(suitable for interdisciplinary teaching)
• Change
• Motivation
• Structures
• Conflict
• Diversity
• Equilibrium
• Context
• Interdependence
• Patterns
• Perspective

skills. For example, "effective collaboration" is an important skill for students working on a group project, but for true collaboration to take place, students need to come to important understandings about the nature of collaboration. They need to understand the importance of facilitating the contributions of all group members, the notion of "active listening," sensitive leadership, an orientation toward problem solving, conflict resolution, and so on. The same is true for many other skills. (See figure 3.2.) These examples also indicate that big ideas include values and habits of mind. As students learn to collaborate effectively (or to "apply the scientific method," "use nonjudgmental observation," "form hypotheses," etc.), they also learn to develop skill and discipline-appropriate values and attitudes, such as "tolerance for ambiguity," "social accountability," "commitment to the pursuit of truth," or "sociocultural awareness." Although not all of these ideas will ultimately be reflected in a course's grading system, an effective course has to be structured with such enabling skills and attitudes in mind.

How to Establish Priorities

So how do we go about selecting the big ideas for a course? (See figures 3.2 and 3.3 for examples of discipline-specific big ideas.) When selecting big ideas, the questions to ask include: Is this idea relevant for this particular course level? How well does it fit in with the goals of the curriculum? How can I connect the various big ideas I choose for the course? In case of a Gen-Ed course: Is this idea equally relevant for majors and nonmajors, or is it only relevant for majors? Certain big ideas might be crucial for someone starting off in a discipline, but of marginal interest for students never planning to move beyond this one course. The selection of big ideas should be based on a rationale that is guided by the discipline itself and what experts consider to be at the core of the discipline and the goals and values of the institution and the program.

Big ideas characterize a discipline. This does not necessarily imply that they have to be unique to one discipline. Some big ideas could, in fact, be shared by several disciplines and thus connect fields with each other. For example, "the scientific method" as a big idea is shared across the natural sciences and even with paradigms in certain social sciences. This makes it particularly relevant for General Education courses, because students can compare similarities as well as differences in the ways disciplines use this big idea, which ultimately allows for more transfer of understanding.

How many big ideas should a course try to address? The answer will depend on the complexity of the ideas, but generally speaking, the reason for starting off with big ideas in the course design process is to limit the universe of what to cover. Two or three big ideas can be perfectly sufficient for a course, because in Step 2, each big idea will be examined for typically more than one "enduring understanding," and in Step 3 those understandings can further be divided into different learning outcomes. Three big ideas could, therefore, easily generate six, nine, or more learning outcomes, which could quickly exceed what a course can meaningfully address in one semester. (See Chapter 3 Graph).

Deriving Enduring Understandings

Connecting Big Ideas With Student Horizons

Although big ideas are determined by the discipline and are student-independent, the second step for determining meaningful learning outcomes must be related to the overall level of sophistication that can be expected of the students in a given course. Enduring understandings are dependent on what Wiggins and McTighe (2005) call "a developmental reality that muddies the distinction between facts and understandings" (p. 136). Experts in a given field might believe facts are what once used to be hard-won understandings by the scholars that went before them. Instructors have to put themselves in the proverbial shoes of their students to determine which commonly accepted insights in their discipline they have yet to uncover, making problematic what might otherwise too easily pass as factual knowledge. The enduring understandings selected for a course are therefore related to the students' prior experience.

Which Understandings Are Enduring?

McTighe and Wiggins (2004) provide several pages of examples for enduring understandings arranged by disciplines. Here are some excerpts:

Art: The greatest artists often break with established traditions and techniques to better express what they see and feel.

Business: Patterns of consumption inform production and marketing decisions.

Economics: Relative scarcity may lead to trade and economic interdependence or to conflict.

Geography: The topography, climate, and natural resources of a region influence the culture, economy, and lifestyle of its inhabitants.

Government: Democratic governments must balance the rights of individuals with the common good.

History: History involves interpretation; historians can and do disagree.

Mathematics: Statistical analysis and data display often reveal patterns that may not be obvious.

Philosophy: Ethicists disagree on whether the results of an action or a person's intentions matter most in judging the morality of actions.

Science: Correlation does not ensure causality.

Teacher Ed.:   The need for behavior management is reduced when teaching is engaging and meaningful to the learners. (McTighe & Wiggins, 2004, pp. 108–110, printed with permission of publisher)

For examples from not only different disciplines but also different grade levels, compare Lynn Erickson's list (Erickson, 2007, pp. 53–55).

A formal distinction between big ideas and enduring understandings is immediately obvious. Whereas the big ideas within the disciplines are often encapsulated in one or two word terms (e.g., *Equity, Nature vs. Nurture, Scientific Method, Natural Selection*), enduring understandings are expressed in whole sentences. They are best stated as propositions that might start off with the tacit phrase: *"Students should understand that . . ."* (Wiggins & McTighe, 2005, p. 136). Key aspects include the following. An enduring understanding:

- Is an important inference drawn from the experience of experts.
- Refers to transferable ideas having enduring value beyond a specific topic.
- Involves abstract ideas that are often counterintuitive or easily misunderstood.
- Is best acquired by having learners discover it for themselves by solving real-world problems in realistic settings.
- Summarizes important strategic principles in skill areas (Wiggins & McTighe, 2005, pp. 128–129).

There are two reasons for calling these understandings "enduring"; they have withstood the test of time and have proven useful across contexts and cultures, and they are what students should take away from their studies long after a given course has ended. Because of their ability to connect topics, they help learners make sense of what otherwise might merely be isolated bits of knowledge that are never applied and are easily forgotten. Enduring understandings typically emerge within a specific discipline, but they often reveal similarities with other disciplines, which makes interdisciplinary work and understanding possible.

Determining Learning Outcomes

How General and How Specific Should They Be?

Big ideas provide the broad topography of what is most important in a given discipline. Selected for a specific course, they represent the first act of focusing on the broad areas the course should address. Enduring understandings narrow down the terrain even further by identifying the most meaningful insights related to these big ideas that are particularly appropriate to the intellectual level and background of the students at a certain course or program level. The learning outcomes that I am proposing as a third step, narrow down yet again the learning that is to take place in the course. Wherever possible, determining learning outcomes should be done not just in view of students' overall intellectual level, but also in terms of their experiential background, what interests them, as well as the barriers they typically encounter in this course. (See the following chapter on critical thinking.) Learning outcomes should be formulated with a view toward the key performance tasks students will be asked to engage in to demonstrate that they have mastered the learning outcome(s). What is it that they should be able to do with their enduring understandings that highlights key aspects of the big ideas in the discipline?

Examples From Specific Courses

The following list gives examples of meaningful learning outcomes from a number of different disciplines:

Political Science: Students can make an accurate and engaging oral presentation analyzing one current issue in American foreign policy. (Huba & Freed, 2000, p. 110)

Psychology: Students can prepare a written summary and interpretation of standardized test results. (Huba & Freed, 2000, p. 110)

Environmental Science: Students will be able to articulate the responsibility of the individual in the sustainable management of energy, soil, water, and plants. (Huba & Freed, 2000, p. 109)

History:	Enable students to evaluate an unfamiliar event in its historical context. Reconstruct an unfamiliar historical event from different viewpoints or a familiar historical event from a new viewpoint. Seek out and evaluate information about an unfamiliar historical event. (Tewksbury & Macdonald, 2005)
Art:	Enable students to go to an art museum and evaluate the technique of an unfamiliar work of art. Evaluate an unfamiliar work in its historical context. Evaluate a work in the context of a particular artistic genre, school, or style. (Tewksbury & Macdonald, 2005)
Mathematics:	Enable students to evaluate statistical claims in the popular press/advertising. Analyze applications of calculus in unfamiliar situations. Solve unfamiliar real-world problems in science/engineering. (Tewksbury & Macdonald, 2005)
Education:	Enable students to design classroom activities for students that are consistent with educational theory and the science of learning. (Tewksbury & Macdonald, 2005)
Geology:	Analyze the modern geologic processes in an unfamiliar area and assess potential hazards to humans (which is different from recalling those covered in class). (Tewksbury & Macdonald, 2005)
American Literature:	Write a poem that uses imagery and structure typical of early 19th century American poets. (Suskie, 2004, p. 84)
Chemistry:	Theorize what is likely to happen when two chemicals are combined, and justify the theory. (Suskie, 2004, p. 84)
Accounting:	Identify an audit problem in a financial statement and recommend ways to address it. (Suskie, 2004, p. 84)
Educational Psychology:	Develop a personal study strategy that makes the most of one's learning style. (Suskie, 2004, p. 85)

Given these examples of meaningful learning outcomes, let us try to summarize what characteristics they need to incorporate to provide appropriate guidance for a course, its students, and the instructor. I am incorporating here descriptions found in Tewksbury and Macdonald (2005), Huba and Freed (2000), Suskie (2004), and Stiehl and Lewchuk (2002):

_dent-focused: Outcomes should be phrased from the perspective of what students will be able *to do after* they have successfully completed the course or program. For example, "By the end of this course, students will be able to design/analyze/compose/compare and contrast/ etc." It's important to look past the tasks students are to perform while still in the course, because we don't want to educate students merely to pass our tests.

2. Emphasis on higher-order thinking skills: Don't just expect students to "understand" or "remember" content. Challenge them to learn how to *do* something with the knowledge they are to acquire, but also to anticipate barriers they are likely to encounter in the course. (See chapter 4.) Outcomes must be challenging enough to direct students through the whole course. It can be helpful to consult a taxonomy of different types of thinking skills to avoid outcomes that are too one-dimensional.

3. Measurable: Make sure that achievement of the learning outcomes can be measured in some form, whether it is in the form of a test, a paper, a presentation, performance, and so on. Outcomes should be phrased with a view toward possible products students might provide as evidence of their learning.

4. Concrete: Sometimes syllabi seem to express merely some general hopes instructors have for what students should get out of a course, for example "develop an interest in lifelong learning," "show a love for the discipline," or "demonstrate critical thinking abilities." Such broad goals violate the previous point—make outcomes measurable. For an outcome to be measurable, it needs to be sufficiently concrete that criteria can be applied for distinguishing higher from lower levels of performance. Students should have an idea of the instructor's expectations for a course as they read the learning outcomes. Using concrete action words can help. Here are some examples from Suskie (2004): *Make appropriate inferences—Design an experiment—Systematically analyze and solve problems—Present original interpretations—Critically evaluate the effectiveness of—Use gender as an analytical category to critique,* and so on.

   However, there might be occasions when it is more useful to ask students to "understand," "become aware of," or "appreciate." In those cases, it is important that you define those broad terms more specifically. For example: "Become aware of . . ." might include: "Describe which aspects of the issue you have never considered important and recognize possible misconceptions you held about this issue."

Some additional characteristics are worth considering. The literature frequently refers to Bloom's taxonomy and its six levels of cognitive operations (knowledge, comprehension, application, analysis, synthesis, and evaluation) to propose an extra layer of dimensions that course outcomes should take into account. The idea behind this is that course outcomes should not stop at the lower levels of learning (knowledge, comprehension, and application), but venture into the more advanced realms of cognition by challenging students to analyze, synthesize, and evaluate the concepts and ideas of a discipline.

Linking Them With Different "Facets of Understanding"

I prefer Wiggins and McTighe's over Bloom's taxonomy, because, even if one combines Bloom's cognitive and affective taxonomies into one, his dimensions of human learning seem more logic-driven and mechanical than guided by psychological processes. Dee Fink (2003, pp. 29–32) pointed out the same issue when he created a taxonomy that makes room for "the human dimension," "caring," and "learning how to learn," thereby significantly expanding the realm of learning. Similarly, Wiggins and McTighe, on the other hand, have created a set of six "facets of understanding" that focus more on the sense-making rather than the purely analytical aspects of human knowledge. The authors explain these facets in detail (2005, pp. 84–104) and with discipline-specific illustrations (2004, pp. 155–166). In the following, I provide a brief summary of the six facets in comparison and contrast to Bloom's categories. It would seem beneficial to refer to those facets of understanding when crafting the learning outcomes for a given course.

- Explanation: connecting events, actions, and ideas to generalizations or principles.
  Explanation is in fact similar to Bloom's "comprehension" category. It clearly requires more than mere knowledge of facts. The learner needs to understand the meaning of those facts and be able to infer how things are connected and why they function the way they do.
- Interpretation: telling meaningful stories or offering reasonable translations.
  This category cannot be found in Bloom's taxonomies. His "analysis," "synthesis," and "evaluation" are operations that assume a largely detached relationship between the learner and what is learned. Interpretation is more concerned about the significance of the subject of investigation, its worth to the learner or to other people.
- Application: effectively using and adapting what we know in diverse contexts.

This category is the only verbatim match between Bloom and Wiggins and McTighe. It requires the learner to be able to use a concept or skill in a new context or a novel situation. The learner thereby shows that he or she has truly understood the material. Wiggins and McTighe push this one step further by calling for real-life, "authentic" problems that ask students to exhibit the same skills that professionals have to apply in the real world.

- Perspective-taking: seeing points of view through critical eyes.
  More than the previous three categories, perspective-taking moves us into what Bloom calls the affective domain. The closest in his schema is the "receiving phenomena" category. In order to be ready to receive phenomena, people have to show awareness and the willingness to be open to others. Wiggins and McTighe's term seems more to the point: Complex phenomena typically have multiple points of view. Those who truly want to understand them need to take other people's perspectives into account.

- Empathy: finding value in what others might find odd.
  Bloom uses the more abstract term of *valuing*, which might simply imply acceptance of objects or behaviors, or it might go beyond that and include a state of commitment to others. For Wiggins and McTighe, empathy enables a different form of insight, one that can only come with engagement. "It is the disciplined attempt of trying to find what is plausible, sensible, or meaningful in the ideas and actions of others, even if those ideas and actions are puzzling or off-putting" (2005, p. 99).

- Self-knowledge: showing metacognitive awareness.
  At the writing of Bloom's cognitive and affective taxonomies, the term *metacognition* had not yet become the important psychological category it is today. None of his affective dimensions comes close enough to addressing the significance of self-knowledge for understanding one's social environment. Self-knowledge, or metacognition, has a reflective connotation. Unless learners are inclined to critically look at themselves first and recognize their own limitations and blind spots, their worldviews will be seriously flawed.

To get back to the task of systematically deriving learning outcomes, instructors frequently wonder how many learning outcomes are enough for a course. It is important to remember that the funnel approach of deriving outcomes from enduring understandings and big ideas serves, among other purposes, to avoid overloading the course with too much detail. Even this funnel procedure can easily generate too many outcomes if instructors don't exercise restraint when identifying multiple items at each level. In addition, keep in mind that a learning outcome that is not assessed in the course is virtually invisible for students. Creating assessment activities for twelve or more outcomes soon leads to overburdening one's teaching agenda. I recommend keeping between five and ten learning outcomes that are sufficiently distinct for faculty and students to remember and recognize as important.

Figure 3.3 illustrates this with a course I taught a number of years ago, for which I have now generated a set of big ideas, enduring understandings, and learning outcomes. *Each of the following chapters will add further elements to this table until it all comes together as a complete course design document in chapter 9.*

At the time I created this course, I was still following the traditional approach of selecting learning outcomes by themselves rather than deriving them from big ideas and enduring understandings. By comparing my new with my old outcomes, readers will notice the difference in quality between the two approaches. The old outcomes read:

> By the end of this course, students should be able to:
>
> 1. Differentiate between major motivation-theoretical concepts.
> 2. Identify problems and implications of different motivation-theoretical approaches.
> 3. Use motivation-theoretical concepts as a springboard for raising questions relevant for their own lives and future professions.
> 4. Use motivation-theoretical concepts for problem solving in real-world situations.
> 5. Identify motivational principles that have particular potential for guiding their own behavior.
>
> (Syllabus for "Theories of Motivation," Fall 2000)

The old outcomes did avoid the pitfall of focusing on the lower levels of learning by requiring students to compare and contrast, identify problems, and apply theory to real-world situations. But there was an unfortunate lack of differentiation between outcomes 1 and 2 and outcomes 3 through 5. The former ask for abstract distinctions between theories. The latter expect students to find applicability of the theories within the students' everyday lives. This redundancy is not uncommon when learning outcomes are simply chosen without first defining a larger context.

The new outcomes have more definition because they are identified as aspects of a bigger train of thought. For example, outcome #1 (see figure

3.1) is not merely self-awareness of previously unconscious tendencies, but self-awareness of external and internal causes of behavior. Outcome #2 is not merely an explanation for the effectiveness of cognitive behavior intervention, but also a reflection on how emotion and cognition interact in controlling people's behaviors. The new outcomes also incorporate five of the six "facets of understanding": Self-knowledge (1 and 6), Explanation (2 and 5), Perspective-taking (3), Empathy (4), and Application (7). And distinguishing the learning outcomes by facets of understanding also helps separate them more clearly from each other.

Figure 3.3 illustrates how to move from big ideas to enduring understandings and learning outcomes. The examples are from three different disciplines—biology, women's studies, and earth science—each providing one big idea, two related enduring understandings, and one learning outcome for each of the understandings.

Finally, let us summarize the various aspects that provide definition to a set of effective learning outcomes. Figure 3.4 can be used as a checklist to make sure everything has been properly considered when creating the basic framework for an academic course.

FIGURE 3.3
Examples of Moving From Big Ideas to Enduring Understandings and Learning Outcomes

BIOLOGY

Big Idea	The Scientific Method
Related Enduring Understandings	1. Science is a process. The more experiments a hypothesis has survived, the more it tends to be accepted.
	2. We learn as much from failure as we do from success.
Related Learning Outcomes	1. Students will be able to contrast the levels of scientific knowledge behind a hypothesis, theory, and a law (noting that even laws are not infallible), and define each from a scientific experiment.
	2. Students will be able to outline the steps of the scientific method for each lab, generate predictions, and maintain the distinction between predicted and observed results, even if the lab experiment fails to produce the expected results.

WOMEN'S STUDIES

Big Idea	Social institutions
Related Enduring Understandings	1. Societal institutions are not separate entities—rather they are interlocking systems and domains of power that work together to produce particular patterns of domination and oppression, advantage or privilege and disadvantage.
	2. Social institutions are sites of power that are organized and operate via the intersections of race, class, gender, sexual orientation, immigration status, abilities, etc.
Related Learning Outcomes	1. Students will be able to observe and examine the inequities of social institutions (e.g., in the media) and describe how the injustices affect women's lives.
	2. Students will be able to analyze social institutions and social relationships and understand how power circulates within and across those systems.

EARTH SCIENCE

Big Idea	Relativity of time and space (The scale is more vast compared to everyday experiences.)
Related Enduring Understandings	1. The Earth changes over time and has a history of development (e.g., climate changes, positions of continents change, etc.).
	2. (Earth Science relies on comprehension of, and ability to move among, very disparate scales of time and space.) The disparity between human perspectives and geologic perspectives of time and space is what constitutes the difference between an event being viewed as a "catastrophe" or as a "normal" process.
Related Learning Outcomes	1. Analyze maps illustrating the distribution of fossils, past glaciations, and current locations of volcanoes and seismic activity, and formulate a hypothesis to explain the patterns you observed.
	2. Analyze a geologic cross section and interpret the sequence of geologic events that produced those features.

FIGURE 3.4
Checklist for Effective Learning Outcomes

INDIVIDUAL OUTCOMES

Factor: Appropriateness of B.I. (Big Idea), E.U. (Enduring Understanding), and L.O. (Learning Outcome)

1. B.I.s and E.U.s are related to the institution's and the program's mission and values
2. B.I. is crucial for both discipline and course level
3. E.U. is crucial for discipline, course level, and students' expected levels of intellectual development
4. L.O. addresses an important aspect of the E.U. (and represents an engaging challenge for students)

Factor: Proper phrasing of L.O.

1. Student-focused
2. Measurable (what student is able to do after course)
3. Higher-order thinking
4. Phrased with the facets of understanding in mind
5. Concrete action words OR
6. Fuzzy terms defined

SET OF OUTCOMES

Factor: Total number

1. Limits number of B.I.s to 2–5
2. Limits number of E.U.s to 4–8
3. Limits number of L.O.s to 5–10

Factor: Number of facets addressed by outcomes

1. Address more than one facet, if feasible
2. Address at least one of the perspective, empathy, or self-knowledge facets, if feasible

CRITICAL THINKING

Intellectual Development

Learned
Misconceptions

Habits of Mind

Complex Reasoning

REMOVING BARRIERS TO CRITICAL THINKING

OVERVIEW

SIGNIFICANCE OF CRITICAL THINKING

- Critical thinking isn't just for upper-level classes

LAY DEFINITIONS OF CRITICAL THINKING

- The critical thinking that instructors assume is implied in their courses

THE CONFUSING STATE OF THE CRITICAL THINKING LITERATURE

- How many characteristics does critical thinking have?
- Critical thinking in different disciplines

NEED FOR TEACHING CRITICAL THINKING

- Is critical thinking acquired "naturally"?
- How college students have changed

BARRIER 1: INTELLECTUAL DEVELOPMENT

- How students' thinking about learning evolves
- How these developmental orientations affect students' learning behaviors

BARRIER 2: HABITS OF MIND

- How intellectual habits affect learning
- Which intellectual habits are important for critical thinking?

BARRIER 3: MISCONCEPTIONS

- Why learning often requires "unlearning" first
- The typical misconceptions that plague various disciplines

BARRIER 4: COMPLEX REASONING

- Why thinking/understanding is deeper than knowing
- Which dimensions of thinking are critical?

CONCLUSION

Significance of Critical Thinking

Critical Thinking Isn't Just for Upper-Level Classes

As shown in the previous chapter, the learning outcomes for a course are defined in a language that denotes challenges for the student. No matter what the course level, outcomes should require learners to go beyond the mere acquisition of facts; learning outcomes should stimulate students' thinking abilities. We do not subscribe to what is occasionally described as the purpose of introductory or General Education courses: Students first have to acquire the factual knowledge base of a discipline before they can apply critical-thinking skills to this base in the higher-level classes. Reserving critical thinking for upper-level students is equivalent to postponing education until a person is already educated. Any introduction of new subject matter should involve higher-order thinking skills from the beginning and, clearly, virtually all faculty agree that critical thinking skills are required in all their courses. One might say that critical thinking is the main intended learning outcome in any college course.

Lay Definitions of Critical Thinking

The Critical Thinking That Instructors Assume Is Implied in Their Courses

Nevertheless, one will find significant discrepancies in how faculty define "critical thinking" in their courses. In fact, such definitions tend to range widely across various dimensions of student performance, with some seeming to be only marginally related to the concept. The following is a brief sample:

- "Written observations based on readings."
- "Good answers on exams."
- "Clear in-class articulation of topics."
- "Passing performance on exams."
- "Response papers to articles on language myths [in a linguistics class]. These require summarizing, presenting author's arguments, etc."
- "I look for evidence of critical thinking in the types of questions students ask as well as in the thoughtfulness with which they complete their written assignments. There is clearly a qualitative difference between just getting the 'correct' answer versus a thoughtful one."

What tends to emerge in such impromptu answers is that critical thinking produces more clarity in what a student says or writes; it makes use of assigned readings so that students can build a more informed argument. It is best measured in writing, especially reflective writing, in which students have to summarize, synthesize, and present their own perspectives, and it is visibly better thinking than merely coming up with correct answers. The degree of thoughtfulness generated by an act of critical thinking makes a qualitative difference that is immediately apparent to the trained eye.

Although the above reactions might typically accompany acts of critical thinking, they are hardly operational definitions that would be helpful in teaching students what we want them to do or how we want them to do it. Giving students any of those definitions of critical thinking would hardly provide useful information for those who think college is all about memorizing facts and identifying the correct answers on multiple-choice exams.

The Confusing State of the Critical Thinking Literature

How Many Characteristics Does Critical Thinking Have?

Quite frankly, given the bewildering array of definitions, categorization schemes, and philosophies found in the literature on critical thinking, it can be rather difficult to come up with descriptions that are clear and helpful. One of the more comprehensive websites on critical thinking (www.aus think.org/critical/pages/definitions.html) lists at least a dozen internationally known authorities of different persuasion, and Jenny Moon (2007), in her recent review of the field, describes six systematically different approaches to conceptualizing critical thinking: (1) Focus on logic, (2) listing of component skills, (3) discipline-specific approaches, (4) personal dispositions, (5) developmental approaches, and (6) approaches that take an overview.

Not surprisingly then, each major theoretician has a set of frameworks he or she claims are crucial for understanding the breadth and depth of critical thinking. To illustrate this, my favorite critical thinking authors, Richard Paul and Linda Elder (2001), distinguish the following dimensions:

- Seven aspects (or habits of mind) of becoming a "fair-minded" thinker
- Six developmental stages of thinking
- Eight universal elements of reasoning

- Nine standards for thinking
- Six dimensions in the logic of decision-making
- Seven dimensions of problem-solving
- Eight pathological tendencies of the mind
- Eight fundamentals of ethical reasoning
- Eleven key ideas of strategic thinking

Critical Thinking in Different Disciplines

Although one might appreciate the distinctions made in such multifaceted approaches, it is doubtful that instructors would be able to translate those distinctions into practical guidelines by which they could teach, especially if we consider the variety of disciplines that college instructors deal with. One of the claims these theorists have made about critical thinking is that it is context-specific. That means that although there are generic skills that are important to foster across disciplines, critical thinking in English literature has different characteristics than critical thinking in anthropology or chemistry or geography. Unfortunately, the critical thinking theorists have not made too many inroads into exploring what these differences are. Probably the strongest effort made to date in this direction comes from Janet Gail Donald's book *Learning to Think: Disciplinary Perspectives* (2002). But even her empirical investigation into thinking processes in various disciplines falls short of providing concrete guidelines to instructors of what to do in their courses.

Need for Teaching Critical Thinking

Is Critical Thinking Acquired "Naturally"?

People might ask why critical thinking needs to be taught at all. Generations of students have learned to develop it "naturally" in the course of going through college. Their faculty modeled it—not necessarily by design—as they taught them which questions to ask and which distinctions to make in their field. Eventually the students adopted the discipline-specific modes of thinking because the discussions with their instructors and peers helped them internalize the appropriate patterns of looking at the subject of their discipline.

How College Students Have Changed

That is certainly a valid argument. Many important skills tend to be learned along the way by immersing oneself repeatedly in the discourse of a discipline. Curious students can pick up on these without necessarily being taught on purpose. However, one difference between today's college students and the college students of a generation ago is that in 2005, a total of 69% of all high school graduates were entering higher education right after finishing high school, whereas in the 1960s, only 45% were doing so (National Center for Education Statistics, 2006). Many college freshmen entering the lower-tier colleges are significantly worse-prepared for college than the average freshman thirty years ago. Large numbers are first-generation students from low-income backgrounds. Increasing numbers of our high school students did not grow up in the United States, creating language barriers formerly not encountered in college. In inner cities, students come from schools that are often ill-equipped to deal with the problems those students are facing in their neighborhoods. Even the better-prepared students tend to see higher education as just one priority among several competing ones that they juggle while going to college. In other words, the social makeup of our college student populations has shifted considerably, and the notion of relative leisure and focus that college students might have devoted to their studies several decades ago no longer exists.

Given the central role of critical thinking in higher education and given the changed makeup of our student populations, we cannot leave the acquisition of critical thinking to chance. In fact, course design needs to make it a centerpiece of planning, and we need to plan it from the perspectives of all that can go wrong with it. Research over the last several decades has uncovered a number of systematic barriers that stand in the way of people becoming critical thinkers. Unless these barriers are addressed in course design, the chances of our students becoming conceptual learners are greatly diminished. The following pages describe four of the biggest barriers and culminate in two tables: one that illustrates the four barriers with current student beliefs and behaviors, and a second one that shows common barriers related to the learning outcomes of the Theories of Motivation course.

Barrier 1: Intellectual Development

How Students' Thinking About Learning Evolves

Since the 1960s, we have learned some things about student development that nobody previously knew or paid attention to. A number of developmental researchers have demonstrated that poor critical-thinking skills are not merely a result of the cognitive factors of low academic preparedness, but also relate to the fact that true critical thinking requires a particular value

system—one might say, a particular view of the world—
rarely possess. Psychologists have looked at different dimen
ment in young, college-age people. The first psychologist tu ᴗ
liam Perry, who looked at the epistemological development of college students (1970). Because Perry's research was exclusively done with male students, Mary Field Belenky and others (1986) looked at similar issues focusing on women. Marcia Baxter-Magolda (1987) looked at gender-related patterns of intellectual development, and Patricia King and Karen Kitchener (1994) emphasized intellectual and moral development in young adults. Although their findings regarding developmental "positions," "perspectives," "patterns," or "stages" differ, the original characterizations by Perry and Belenky and others illustrate the overall developmental perspective. Joanne Gainen Kurfiss (1988) synthesized the main insights from these two research efforts into four "levels" that can be outlined as follows:

1. DUALISM (Received Knowledge)
   - Knowledge is objective, a collection of discrete facts.
   - Things are either right or wrong, good or bad, black or white, and so on.
   - Learning is simply a matter of acquiring information.
   - The professor is the authority who has all the answers.
   - Students become uneasy if:
     ○ They don't receive important information and the right answers.
     ○ They are asked to state their own opinions or draw their own conclusions.
     ○ They are asked to learn from their peers.
2. MULTIPLICITY (Subjective Knowledge)
   - Knowledge is subjective.
   - Most students gradually acknowledge the existence of unknowns, doubts, and uncertainties, at least in some areas of knowledge.
   - When facts are not known, knowledge is a matter of mere opinion.
   - The majority of college students subscribe to this category of epistemological beliefs.
   - Students complain to their instructor for:
     ○ Criticizing their work (because it's just one opinion against another).
     ○ Failing to make evaluation criteria clear.

3. CONTEXTUAL RELATIVISM (Procedural Knowledge)
   - Students realize that "opinions" differ in quality and that good opinions are supported with reasons.
   - What counts as true depends on (is relative to) the frame of reference used to evaluate the phenomenon in question.
   - Fewer than half of college seniors subscribe to this epistemological perspective.
   - Students complain to their instructor:
     - That the more they analyze complexities, the less able they are to make decisions or draw conclusions.
4. COMMITMENT IN RELATIVISM (Constructed Knowledge)
   - Knowledge is constructed, that is, ultimately, individuals must take a position and make commitments, even though they have no external assurances of "correctness."
   - Constructed knowledge integrates knowledge from others with the "inner truth" of experience and personal reflection.
   - Constructed knowledge includes the *self* in the knowing process, becoming passionately engaged in the search for understanding. These learners are committed to nurturing rather than criticizing ideas.

How These Developmental Orientations Affect Students' Learning Behaviors

The levels represent convictions and belief systems students hold that are the lenses through which they view learning and teaching. Those lenses turn out to be systematic barriers to students' learning and critical thinking. As they progress through college, their intellectual perspectives might gradually become more sophisticated until they reach level four, but empirical research into the functioning of upper-level students suggests that many of them have not progressed beyond the second or third level.

Many instructors will agree that entering college students frequently function at the first two levels described above, with the indicated restrictions for their functioning in the classroom. They tend to have a simplistic view of knowledge and learning that is often reinforced by teaching and textbooks that emphasize the acquisition of facts and by multiple-choice exams that suggest there is always one right answer. Poor teaching leads to misconceptions of learning, thereby creating a barrier for critical thinking that college has to work hard to move out of the way. To give critical thinking a chance, learners who have settled into a binary concept of knowledge have to be moved out of their comfort zone. That is bound to be met with some resistance.

Barrier 2: Habits of Mind

How Intellectual Habits Affect Learning

Another dimension that is related to human development is the notion of intellectual habits or dispositions to learning that we hope will come with a quality education. Wiggins calls it one of the five goals of education (1998, p. 72), one that by definition only develops over a long period of time and is not readily found in every student. Paul and Elder (2001) see a fundamental tendency in humans to be self-centered rather than what they call "fair-minded." This tendency to look at everything around ourselves from merely our own perspective is a major threat to critical thinking. The habits of mind designed to defeat this egocentric view are characterized by a disposition to be fair and leave behind one's selfish interest.

Which Intellectual Habits Are Important for Critical Thinking?

Paul and Elder distinguish seven different intellectual habits that they consider crucial for the critical thinker: intellectual humility, courage, empathy, integrity, perseverance, autonomy, and confidence in reason. (See figure 4.1. Italicized statements are my elaborations.) These illustrate the point that critical thinking is not merely about skills; it is also about an attitude that shapes a person's stance toward his or her natural and social environment. In other words, critical thinking is also about building character or helping a student become an "educated" person.

Barrier 3: Misconceptions

Why Learning Often Requires "Unlearning" First

In his 1991 book *The Unschooled Mind*, Howard Gardner summarizes some of the research that has been done on systematic and discipline-specific misconceptions that students bring to college. He traces those misconceptions back to conflicts between the set of theories and scripts that students developed before entering school (theories about mind, matter, life, and self) and the new forms of knowing that are introduced to them as they go through

FIGURE 4.1
Intellectual Habits of Critical Thinkers

Fair-mindedness entails a consciousness of the need to treat all viewpoints alike, without reference to one's own feelings or selfish interests. It is based on an awareness of the fact that we, by nature, tend to prejudge the views of others, placing them into "favorable" (agrees with us) and "unfavorable" (disagrees with us) categories. We tend to give less weight to contrary views than to our own. Fair-mindedness requires us to develop:

1. *Intellectual Humility*
   Awareness of one's biases, one's prejudices, the limitations of one's viewpoint, and the extent of one's ignorance. *(e.g., Many U.S. and other Western students consider their ways of life—competition, individualism, materialism, democratic forms of government, nuclear family arrangements, work ethic—superior to non-Western values and living arrangements. Their biases have a profound impact on their understanding of important concepts in the social sciences, the arts, and the humanities.)*

2. *Intellectual Courage*
   Consciousness of the need to face and fairly address ideas, beliefs, or viewpoints toward which one has strong negative emotions and to which one has not given a serious hearing; the recognition that ideas that society considers dangerous or absurd are sometimes rationally justified—in whole or in part. *(e.g., Any culture has its set of taboos that also affect scientific discourse. Recent examples include stem cell research, gay marriage, Muslim radicalism or any other radicalism for that matter, global warming, atheism, affirmative action, assisted suicide, and pornography. It takes courage to openly investigate any potentially rational roots for any of these controversial behaviors and beliefs.)*

3. *Intellectual Empathy*
   Awareness of the need to imaginatively put oneself in the place of others so as to genuinely understand them. *(Old paradigms in the social sciences often treated their research "subjects" as variables that were to be looked at with no emotional involvement in order to guarantee "objectivity." Nowadays, many social scientists are taking a different approach to understanding social environments. To thoroughly understand others' behaviors and intentions, young scholars need to acquire the ability to take their research subjects' perspective, requiring a degree of personal identification previously denounced as a contamination of the research process. Similar abilities have always been considered a precondition for producing and appreciating good literature and other types of art.)*

4. *Intellectual Integrity*
   Recognition of the need to be true to one's own thinking and to hold oneself to the same standards one expects others to meet. It also means to honestly admit discrepancies and inconsistencies in one's own thought and action. *(e.g., Cutting corners, plagiarizing, and cheating have become pervasive not only in college, but also in graduate school and beyond. Society's expectations for accelerated output in every realm of life, including academia, can put tremendous pressure on students to impress with productivity at the expense of academic rigor and relevance. Admitting shortcomings in one's thinking requires just as much courage as fairly addressing viewpoints with which one vehemently disagrees; see point 2.)*

5. *Intellectual Perseverance*

   The disposition to work one's way through intellectual complexities despite the frustration inherent in the task. *(Many students in our current school system learn to avoid those things that seem too difficult: "Engineering is too tedious," "Math is too hard," and "A PhD in Accounting doesn't pay off." Delaying gratification for the fruit of one's labor is as hard for a student as it is for a child to wait for dessert. This applies also to the daily struggle with intellectual tasks. Many students ask for simple answers and are suspicious when their discipline has not yet produced answers to difficult issues, or when those answers remain ambiguous.)*

6. *Confidence in Reason*

   The belief that one's own higher interests and those of humankind at large will be best served by giving the freest play to reason, by encouraging people to come to their own conclusions by developing their own rational faculties; faith that, with proper encouragement and cultivation, people can learn to think for themselves. *(Confidence in reason is also confidence in others. It is a pedagogical principle that good teachers live by. Students should not be persuaded to adopt their teachers' viewpoints or drilled to approach tasks in one particular way only. Complex understanding needs to be nurtured, not forced. Experiencing the freedom and encouragement to solve problems in one's own way helps create intellectual maturity. This includes the freedom to make one's own mistakes and learn from them.)*

7. *Intellectual Autonomy*

   An internal motivation based on the ideal of thinking for oneself; having rational self-authorship of one's beliefs, values, and way of thinking; not being dependent on others for the direction and control of one's thinking. *(The traditional teaching paradigm of telling students what to learn through lecture and textbooks turned students into passive recipients of knowledge. Teachers were the experts whom students trusted to always have the right answers. No thinking for oneself was required. The new learning paradigm puts students in control and makes them accountable for their own learning. Learning theory has discovered diverse learning styles, and motivation theory shows that deep understanding is linked with learner autonomy. The more confident students become in finding their own direction, the more likely they are to develop an integrated understanding of the subjects of their study.)*

(Richard Paul & Linda Elder, 2001)

formal schooling. (See examples in figure 4.2.) New networks of concepts and frameworks and disciplinary ways of looking at the world often contradict students' earlier worldviews, but schools rarely attempt to reconcile what students already think with the thinking that schools try to promote. This jeopardizes true conceptual understanding. "Education for understanding can come about only if students somehow become able to integrate the prescholastic with the scholastic and disciplinary ways of knowing and, when such integration does not prove possible, to suspend or replace the prescholastic ways of knowing in favor of the scholastic forms of knowing" (Gardner, 1991, p. 149). In other words, some of the lay theories and ways of looking at the world that students develop in the first years of their lives have to be unlearned or at least reconsidered from new perspectives before school learning can be successful.

Given the bureaucratic constraints under which they typically operate, schools tend to have a low threshold for taking risks. But risks are exactly what they would have to take to help students overcome their prior understandings in favor of the new disciplinary understandings. Unfortunately, instead of taking risks, schools tend to accept a compromise in which genuine understanding is replaced by "ritualized, rote, or conventionalized performances" (Gardner, 1991, p. 150). This lowers the risk of failures, in which both students and teachers would look bad, and creates the appearance of learning taking place, even though that learning is skin-deep and rarely addresses the disjunctions between intuitive (preschool) and formal school knowledge.

The Typical Misconceptions That Plague Various Disciplines

As students enter college and are faced with in-depth disciplinary studies, their educational history from their early school days (or even beforehand) tends to get in the way. Early intuitive theories and rigid algorithms learned in school can lead to difficulties and systematic misconceptions about phenomena later addressed by academic disciplines. "Each discipline, and perhaps each subdiscipline, poses its own peculiar forms of difficulties, its own constraints that must be tackled" (Gardner, 1991, p. 151). This leads to distortions that threaten the understanding of key conceptual frameworks. Figure 4.2 briefly lists some of the types of misconceptions and stereotypes that Gardner describes in his book. With the exception of psychology, I have added my own labels to each misconception to illustrate the dimensions represented by various misconceptions.

By now a large body of research exists, especially in science teaching (Barke, Hazari, & Yitbarek, 2009; Rose, Minton, & Arline, 2006; Stepans, 2003), but also in psychology (Amsel, Frost, & Johnston, n.d.; Kujawski & Kowalski, 2004; Lilienfeld, Lynn, Ruscio, & Beyerstein, 2009; Ruscio, 2005), history and other disciplines (Donovan & Bransford, 2005; Gardner, 1991). Entire websites with detailed lists of misconceptions (see New York Science Teacher; Missouri Department of Elementary and Secondary Education) have been created that document the scale of the problem. These studies show that college students who have taken courses in science and other

FIGURE 4.2
Examples of Misconceptions in the Disciplines

PHYSICS
- *Inappropriate analogies:* In trying to understand a phenomenon like electricity, students draw on available mental models like "flowing water" or "teeming crowds" without seeing their shortcomings. (p. 157)
- *Simplistic explanations:* Differences in seasons are seen as caused by the distance of the earth from the sun, rather than, as is correct, by the angle at which the sun's rays pass through the earth's atmosphere. (p. 155)
- *Naive folk theories:* An object that moves through a curved tube acquires a "momentum" that causes it to continue in curvilinear motion after it emerges from the tube. (Contradicts Newton's laws of motion.) (p. 154)

BIOLOGY
- *Assumption of teleological tendencies:* It is difficult for students to understand the undirected nature of evolution; they prefer to see later-evolving species as in some way better, more closely approximating an ideal of perfection. (pp. 158–159)
- *Simplistic explanations:* When looking at phenomena of evolution, students fail to distinguish between changes that can be observed at a given historical moment and the chances that these changes may be manifest in future generations. They attribute changes to environmental alterations rather than to random processes of mutation and natural selection. (p. 158)
- *Anthropomorphism:* Students are also prone to believe that biological processes reflect the intentions of a living substance. (Parasites are trying to destroy their hosts.) (p. 159)

ECONOMICS
- *Naive folk theories:* "The more they sell, the lower the price should be, because you can still keep the profit the same." (Inconsistent with economic theory.)
- *Overall "halo effect."* Economically good times are always associated with low interest rates. (p. 168)

STATISTICS/PROBABILITY
- *Limited focus:* Faced with two scenarios where students could save $5 on the combined purchase of two items (a $15 calculator minus a $5 rebate plus a $125 jacket—OR—a $125 calculator minus a $5 rebate plus a $15 jacket), students tend to be biased toward the first scenario, in which the rebate on item 1 amounts to 33%, although in both cases they save the exact same total of $5. (p. 170)
- *Psychological interference:* Students tend to ignore statistical principles of probability as soon as a minor biasing factor is introduced into an estimation task. (e.g., "Linda is single, outspoken, and involved in social issues." Which one is more likely to be true about her: (a) "Linda is a bank teller" or (b) "Linda is a bank teller *and* is active in the feminist movement"? Students choose the much less probable answer "b".)

FIGURE 4.2 (Continued)

PSYCHOLOGY
- *"Fundamental attribution error"*: People attribute their own actions to external causes (e.g., environmental factors such as distractions or other's advice), whereas they attribute the same actions by others to internal personality traits (e.g., dishonesty, laziness, or ambition). (p. 171)
- *"Status quo effect"*: People prefer the option they have selected, even when they recognize that another action is superior.
- *"Bias to omit rather than commit"*: People will spurn a vaccine that can occasionally cause harm, even when the chances of harm are trivial as compared with the possibility of harm should the vaccine not be taken. (p. 172)

HISTORY AND LITERARY STUDIES
- *Coherence bias:* An initial bias in dealing with historical or literary texts is to assume that one will necessarily encounter some kind of story or dramatic narrative. (p. 172)
- *Dualism (see* Barrier 1): Many students view history as the ordering of already-known facts into agreed-upon chronologies. For many of them, history *is* facts. (p. 174)
- *Lack of intellectual perseverance (see* Barrier 2): The common approach of not looking for more complex explanations when simpler ones will do biases students toward literal readings and interpretations of texts that miss clues signaling symbolic or allegoric meanings. (p. 174)

disciplines often exhibit the same misconceptions and misunderstandings as students who have never taken such courses (Gardner, 1991, p. 4). In fact, "young adults trained in science . . . exhibit the same misconceptions that one encounters in primary school children" (Gardner, 1991, p. 4). College courses unaware of these systematic shortcomings are not likely to prepare students to become critical thinkers in (or understand the conceptual depths of) their disciplines.

Barrier 4: Complex Reasoning

Why Thinking/Understanding Is Deeper Than Knowing

Purposeful teaching of critical thinking requires a clear sense of the critical thinking dimensions that are relevant for one's course. Although different theories provide varying frameworks, most do agree on the importance of certain key criteria, even if they name them differently or go into varying levels of detail. For most courses, though, a modest set of criteria, as found in many critical-thinking rubrics, will suffice. Our university's General Education Committee created a critical-thinking rubric by adapting a model from Washington State University (http://wsuctproject.wsu.edu/ctr.htm). The following lists the criteria addressed in this rubric:

1. Identifies and explains **issues**
2. Recognizes stakeholders and **contexts** (i.e., cultural/social, educational, technological, political, scientific, economic, ethical, personal experience)
3. Frames personal responses and acknowledges other **perspectives**
4. Identifies and evaluates **assumptions**
5. Identifies and evaluates **evidence**
6. Identifies and evaluates **implications**

The task of identifying the relevant **issues** within a complex, ill-defined scenario is important across many different disciplines. Typical textbook problems are already predefined; the issue to be resolved has been given, the relevant variables are clearly laid out, and the factors leading to a solution are often presented in the boldfaced terms of the currently assigned chapter. That leaves little room for the development of critical thinking. In the real world, however, critical thinking deals with problems or issues that:

1. Can't be described with a high degree of completeness.
2. Have no *single or obvious* solution.
3. Warrant serious human attention. (Huba & Freed, 2000, p. 202)

Similarly, recognizing the variables or stakeholders that create the relevant **context** for an issue is a formidable task in any discipline. Phenomena don't exist by themselves but are part of a larger whole—whether social, technological, or environmental—that is rarely self-evident or conflict-free. This context is what often leads to different **perspectives** in looking at an issue, and each of these perspectives has a certain rationale that makes it more or less viable, useful, or enlightening. None of this is readily available, and the task for the critical-thinker is to unearth these elements sufficiently though never completely.

Which Dimensions of Thinking Are Critical?

Identifying issues, contexts, and perspectives could be some of the most important tasks for students who are still operating at the *dualistic level* of their development. They are used to issues being given and clear-cut, contexts being accidental and largely irrelevant, and perspectives being restricted to right or wrong. When dealing with students in introductory courses, it might therefore be particularly relevant to practice these three dimensions: identifying issues, recognizing relevant contexts, and framing their own and other people's perspectives on the issue.

The other criteria in the rubric deal more with the thinking that is done after the issue has been framed, put in context, and looked at from different perspectives. As people try to resolve an issue, they can't help but make **assumptions** about its nature, how best to approach it, or how it's related to other issues. Assumptions tend to be invisible because they are based on people's ingrained convictions and everyday practices. They therefore appear to be "natural" and unquestionable because they are rooted in the way in which not only one person, but typically his or her whole peer group, has done things for as long as they can remember. And yet, that's exactly why it is important to identify them as such and to evaluate the convictions from which they originate.

Dealing with assumptions must also address students' naive misconceptions about "the way things are" (Barrier #3) that students acquired either in their early education or even before they entered formal schooling. These misconceptions can play such a major role; they have been carried around for so long and have become so ingrained that it is difficult to bring them back to the surface and identify them as something that was actually learned at some point, but based on false assumptions.

Criterion number five, **evidence**, addresses the execution of an attempt at resolving an issue. There are different types of evidence—such as empirical data, expert opinions, theoretical arguments, and personal experiences—that might be relevant in the case. Each of these has different strengths and weaknesses. Evidence might support a person's position, or it might discredit an opposing position. One piece of evidence might not be strong enough to make the case. Often evidence from a variety of sources or angles will be necessary if people are to be convinced of the viability of a problem resolution.

Finally, there are the **implications** of proposing a certain resolution to an issue. A certain approach might resolve an issue, but the consequences of such a resolution might ultimately be detrimental. Solving one problem by creating another one would hardly be desirable. Critical thinking does not look at issues in isolation. Real-world problems usually have multiple resolutions, but some of them might be better in the larger scheme of things than others. Often, the consequences of a problem-resolution might have both positive and negative implications, and it becomes a matter of weighing the implications of multiple approaches before suggesting the least detrimental.

Identifying assumptions, evidence, and implications are tasks particularly relevant for students at developmental levels beyond dualism. *Multiplistic* learners need to recognize that not every argument is just as valid as any other. They need to understand how underlying assumptions can undermine the strength of an argument, and that different types of evidence make one position more viable than another. Especially the *relativistic* learner, who has understood that knowledge is contextual and procedural, will benefit from weighing the implications of a problem solution. Students at this level will be more ready to weigh the pros and cons of one approach versus another one, recognizing that perfect solutions are hardly ever available under real-world conditions.

This concern about students' developmental readiness does not suggest that instructors can only give those tasks to students who match the appropriate developmental level. Students need to be challenged to move beyond their current level of functioning by being confronted with tasks that demand a more sophisticated type of thinking. Combining the skill demands of the critical-thinking rubric with the levels of students' cognitive-epistemological development is only meant to illustrate that different criteria might require faculty to provide different practice opportunities for students to be able to live up to them.

Conclusion

The previous look at systematic barriers to critical thinking was meant to support the importance of teaching critical thinking on purpose rather than just hoping it will develop naturally in today's college classes. Given our student populations—with their baggage of academic underpreparedness, modern-day distractions, and competing life demands—and given developmental mechanisms that tend to get in the way, hoping for critical thinking capacities to emerge without a purposeful design is likely to leave many students stranded. Higher education cannot afford to follow traditional approaches with nontraditional learners.

The barriers and misconceptions described in the previous pages are at the heart of student learning and idea-based course design. Conceptual learning is a matter of moving back and forth between unlearning old beliefs and practices and replacing them with more appropriate understandings of ourselves and our academic discipline. A well-designed course helps students encounter such instances of disequilibrium that lead them to identify unfounded assumptions and discover new modes of thinking. Old ideas have to be discarded before new ideas can take root.

Figure 4.3 illustrates this in more detail by taking the four types of barriers described in this chapter, presenting common subcategories of each, and showing how students in today's classrooms tend to fall short on each one of these subcategories. For example, intellectual perseverance (habit of mind #5) is often jeopardized by a play-it-safe attitude that "avoids challenging tasks so as not to risk making mistakes." Similarly, learned misconception type 1 ("inappropriate analogies") frequently creates a trap for the novice psychology student who believes that any science is after the discovery of objective laws and therefore psychology must be, too.

Figures 9.2 and 9.3 in chapter 9 will demonstrate how the identification of typical student misconceptions helps make the connection between course learning outcomes and the essential questions that guide the learning progress in the course. Student misconceptions are the perfect vehicle for exploring the big ideas and enduring understandings of the course and connecting them with the main performance tasks that engage students in the exploration of the discipline's guiding concepts.

FIGURE 4.3
Examples of Four Categories of Critical Thinking Barriers

Dimensions of Critical Thinking

Intellectual Development Epistemological Beliefs	Habits of Mind	Learned Misconceptions	Complex Reasoning
Dualism: • Knowledge is objective. • There is always a right and wrong answer. • Learning is acquiring information. *Multiplicity:* • Knowledge is subjective. • Definitive knowledge has not yet been found everywhere. • Therefore, knowledge is mere opinion.	1. Intellectual Humility. 2. Intellectual Courage. 3. Intellectual Empathy. 4. Intellectual Integrity. 5. Intellectual Perseverance. 6. Intellectual Autonomy.	1. Inappropriate analogies. 2. Simplistic (e.g., either/or) explanations 3. Naive folk theories. 4. Assumption of teleological tendencies. 5. Coherence bias.	1. What are the issues? 2. What are the contexts, and who are the stakeholders? 3. Which different perspectives exist? 4. What are the underlying assumptions? 5. How good is the evidence? 6. What possible implications do the proposed solutions have?

Contemporary Examples of Barriers to Critical Thinking

Dysfunctional Epistemological Beliefs	Bad Habits of Mind	Misconceptions in Psychology	Poor Reasoning
Dualism: • Learning is separate from writing. • Reading is for remembering, not for understanding. • Learning is rote memorization. • Academic success is based on inborn intelligence. • Therefore, learning happens fast or not at all. • Learning is either fun and easy or hard and boring. *Multiplicity:* • Reflective papers are merely personal opinions. • One learns nothing in student groups because students lack expertise.	1. I know I am exceptional because people have always praised me. 2. When it comes to sensitive issues like race or religion, it is better to stick with politically correct responses. 3. Why should I be slowed down by working with other students? 4. If they become burdensome, I will ignore my standards and obligations. 5. I avoid challenging tasks so as not to risk making mistakes. 6. It is the instructor's job to tell me what to do.	1. Like any other science, psychology is after discovery of objective laws. 2. People can be divided into introverts and extroverts, intrinsically and extrinsically motivated, Type A and Type B personalities, etc. 3. Emotions are biological and cannot be controlled. 4. Over one's lifespan, human development always progresses to higher stages. 5. Adolescents share a set of unique characteristics that distinguishes them from adults.	1. Reacting only to symptoms without considering the underlying issues. 2. Ignoring the contexts and stakeholders influencing a problem. 3. Assuming there is only one "right" way of addressing the issue. 4. Taking statements as value-neutral and a matter of "common sense." 5. Confusing "rhetoric" with evidence. 6. Looking at a problem in isolation, i.e., not seeing that the current problem is connected with other situations.

FROM ENDURING UNDERSTANDINGS
TO GUIDING CONCEPTS

ENDURING UNDERSTANDINGS	MISCONCEPTIONS	ESSENTIAL QUESTIONS	GUIDING CONCEPTS
E.U.1	M.1.1 M.1.2 M.1.3 etc.	E.Q.1.1 E.Q.1.2 E.Q.1.3 etc.	G.C.1.1 G.C.1.2 G.C.1.3 etc.
E.U.2	List of beliefs that interfere with Enduring Understanding #2	List of essential questions that address both the Enduring Understanding #2 and possibly also one or more of the false beliefs	List of guiding concepts that relate to one or more of the essential questions
E.U.3			
E.U.4			

5

CONTENT, PART 1: GUIDING QUESTIONS AND CONCEPTS

OVERVIEW

TOPICS

- What do topics do to course content?
- Why conceptual understanding goes beyond topics

TWO PARTS OF COURSE CONTENT

- The logic of course design: linear vs. circular process
- Why divide the course content chapter into two parts?

ESSENTIAL QUESTIONS

- How to structure course content with an inquiry orientation
- Topical vs. overarching, and open vs. guiding questions

GUIDING CONCEPTS

- How guiding concepts subsume course topics
- Macro- vs. micro-concepts: Breadth vs. depth of understanding

COURSE CONTENT AND CRITICAL THINKING

- How they are connected

Topics

What Do Topics Do to Course Content?

Comparing "traditional" and "backward" course design models, in chapter 2 I emphasized the problem that faculty face in the form of the massive amounts of content that beg to be covered. The only help faculty have for handling those masses of factual content in the traditional model is to subsume them under "topics." This creates some semblance of order, but it doesn't necessarily help reduce the overall volume of facts. After all, there is nothing to keep the number of topics from rising, considering the ever-increasing number of facts that every discipline generates as it continues to grow. Topics are simply a *passive* organization device for facts and take up the second-lowest level in the structure of knowledge, as Lynn Erickson outlined it in her 2002 book on concept-based curriculum design:

LEVEL 5:	Theory
LEVEL 4:	Principle/Generalization
LEVEL 3:	Concepts
LEVEL 2:	Topics
LEVEL 1:	Facts

Why Conceptual Understanding Goes Beyond Topics

Facts and topics are the basis of the knowledge structure, but not until the next three higher levels of these knowledge bits are organized into purposeful networks that create functional connections among them. This has consequences for classroom learning. Erickson (2002, p. 64) provides an example of two curricular units with a similar heading. In the first one, the teaching is organized around topics, whereas in the second one, it revolves around a conceptual framework (or "conceptual lens," as she calls it).

The topic-centered unit is simply an arrangement of subtopics around a central topic, in this case "Media in american society." The subtopics are borrowed from different disciplines and are illustrated in figure 5.1.

Compare that format to a unit on media in american society built around a theme that provides a conceptual framework for relating the various subtopics to each other. The disciplines remain the same, but the content studied is more focused (see figure 5.2).

The knowledge acquired by students in these two different instructional units is from the same disciplines and most likely covers some of the same

FIGURE 5.1
Topic-Centered Unit

MEDIA IN AMERICAN SOCIETY

SOCIAL STUDIES
  • History of media development

SCIENCE
  • Technology of media

POLITICAL SCIENCE/GOVERNMENT
  • Laws governing media

ART/MUSIC
  • Types of media for art/music

VOCATIONAL
  • Types of jobs in media

LITERATURE/MEDIA
  • Documentaries on media
  • Books/articles on media

(Erickson, 2002)

facts. But the organizational frameworks for this knowledge are very different and will likely result in completely different learning outcomes. In the topics-centered unit, content mastery is the aim of instruction. In the concept- or "idea-centered" (Erickson, 2002) unit, it is merely the means. In the former, the learning is shallow, memorization-based, and fragmented. In the latter, the learning is integrated to facilitate students' understanding of key issues. This also follows the distinction made by Wiggins and McTighe (2005) between teaching that simply follows "the logic of the content" versus "the logic of learning the content" (see chapter 2). The logic of the content may be packaged into neat sets of facts and topics, but the logic of learning the content requires making connections across topics so that understanding can be transferred from one area to another within a discipline and across disciplines.

Two Parts of Course Content

At this point, an editorial note is in order. The reader will have noticed that the content chapter is divided into two parts and that these two parts are

FIGURE 5.2
Theme-Centered Unit

MEDIA AS A PERSUASIVE FORCE IN AMERICAN SOCIETY

SOCIAL STUDIES
- Historical development of technology
- Social effects of media persuasion
- Fads, trends
- History of media influence

SCIENCE
- Choices of technology for quality/effect
- Science of technology

POLITICAL SCIENCE/GOVERNMENT
- Privacy issues
- Legal parameters
- Social debate on media limits

ART/MUSIC
- Ads appeal; aesthetics
- Music influence
- Persuasive techniques

VOCATIONAL
- Product videos, ads
- Use of media in sales and marketing
- Resumes—video/portfolio

LITERATURE/MEDIA
- Ads, editorials
- Debates
- News magazines
- Tabloids
- Viewer responsibility

(Erickson, 2002)

interrupted by additional chapters. That might seem odd, especially given the common notion that there is nothing more straightforward about a course than its content. It turns out that nothing about course design is really straightforward. In this book I am trying to simplify the recursive design process as much as possible into a logical progression from one point to the next.

The Logic of Course Design: Linear vs. Circular Process

Unfortunately, as Stiehl and Lewchuk say about course and curriculum planning, "Nothing comes last because it's not a linear process. The only rule we propose is the one that says, 'Outcomes come first.' Everything else comes second" (2005, p. 71). The reason is that outcomes-based course design begins at the end, but then constantly has to make adjustments, because every new part provides more detail and specificity to the overall picture. Wiggins and McTighe (2005) characterize the process by saying, "Designers must begin to think about assessment *before* deciding what and how they will teach" (p. 19). Course outcomes have to be written with an eye on how the students' achievement of these outcomes should best be measured.

However, although "outcomes come first," they, too, might have to be adjusted when it becomes clearer which procedures will be used to assess their achievement. And these assessment procedures will likely have to be adjusted when we have finally decided which learning activities the course content requires for preparing students to do well on the assessments. Each aspect influences all the others. Although we have to start with certain outcomes in mind, the outcomes are also impacted by how they can be assessed, which itself is shaped by the content, which in turn is influenced by the outcomes, and so on (see the curricular alignment graph, figure 2.2). To use an analogy, course design is like building a bridge; it has to be constructed from both ends simultaneously. While working on the big ideas and enduring understandings on one end, the other end must design the tasks that will be used to assess students, as well as the competencies needed to perform these tasks. The remaining two pieces, learning outcomes and course content, have to be carefully adjusted to each other, because they form the centerpiece that connects the two ends and gives the bridge its durability and the course its capacity to educate.

Why Divide the Course Content Chapter Into Two Parts?

So why two parts of the content chapter? Some elements of the content are more directly shaped by the learning outcomes (based on the big ideas and enduring understandings). Other elements of the content are shaped by the assessment, including the practice opportunities needed to help students gain a deep understanding of the content and then measuring to what extent this was accomplished. That is why I divide the content chapter into a first part that is closely linked to how the learning outcomes are derived from the big ideas and enduring understandings, and into a second part that follows how the achievement of outcomes ought to be facilitated and assessed.

Essential Questions

How to Structure Course Content With an Inquiry Orientation

Idea-based course design focuses on conceptual understanding, not factual knowledge. Conceptual understanding involves critical thinking, and critical thinking requires inquiry. That logic is easy to follow up to this point. Sometimes faculty define ambitious learning outcomes and assert the importance of critical thinking in their courses. They subsequently fall into the content acquisition trap and proceed to structure their courses around a sequence of topics that emphasize factual learning rather than conceptual understanding. The challenge is to treat course content as an extension of learning outcomes that are acquired by raising issues, looking for connections, and revealing the big ideas (hence the name "idea-based learning"). If topics cannot be the organizing principle for creating such courses, what else can?

This is where the framework created by big ideas, enduring understandings, and learning outcomes begins to pay off. The enduring understandings in particular provide a handy background for raising essential questions about course content. Posing those questions allows a list of key issues that can guide the content structure of the course to emerge. Here are two examples from the literature on how to draw essential questions from enduring understandings:

Course:	The American Revolution
Enduring Understanding:	Revolution can result from rigidity in an existing system.
Essential Questions:	(a) What factors led to the American Revolution?
	(b) How did the principles of freedom and independence forge the revolutionary movement?
	(c) How does "rigidity" in a social, political, or economic system affect the functioning of the system? (Erickson, 2002, p. 143)

Course:	Statistics
Enduring Understanding:	Statistics can represent or model complex phenomena.
Essential Questions:	(a) What are the limits of mathematical representation and modeling?
	(b) What is "average"?

> (c) How can mathematics help us decide (e.g., in grading, voting, ranking?) (McTighe & Wiggins, 2004, p. 84)

For each discipline, essential questions can be raised that go to the heart of that discipline. McTighe and Wiggins (2004) give some examples:

Arithmetic
- What if we didn't have numbers?
- Can everything be quantified?

Arts
- Where do artists get their ideas?
- How does art reflect, as well as shape, culture?

Geography
- What makes places unique and different?
- How does where we live influence how we live?

History
- Is history the story told by the winners?
- What can we learn from the past?

Literature
- What makes a great book?
- Should a story teach you something?

Music
- How are sounds and silence organized in various musical forms?
- What roles does music play in the world? (pp. 89–90)

What makes for good essential questions? "No question is *inherently* essential" (Wiggins & McTighe, 2005, p. 110). It is all a matter of context. Who is the audience? What is the purpose? Besides context, there are some general criteria to consider. Effective essential questions:

- Cause relevant inquiry into the big ideas and core content.
- Provoke deep thought, lively discussion, and more questions.
- Require students to consider alternatives and justify their answers.
- Stimulate ongoing rethinking of prior lessons.
- Spark meaningful connections with prior learning.

- Create opportunities of transfer to other situations and subjects. (Wiggins & McTighe, 2005, p. 110)

Looking back at the previous chapter on critical thinking, I might add one characteristic. Essential questions can also be framed to address the typical misconceptions that students bring to the discipline. They challenge students to consider the sources of their beliefs as they get in the way of an in-depth understanding of the discipline. In fact, for the earlier courses taught in a discipline, student misconceptions might provide one of the most productive sources for creating essential questions.

Essential questions do not have prefabricated answers that students can memorize. They call on students to think for themselves and uncover their own responses. They are not limited to a topic but require the learner to make connections and transfer what they have learned in one context to related aspects of another context. That is why essential questions are at the heart of critical thinking. A course is built as a continuum of questions that help learners unpack the meaning of the course content for themselves. "Make the 'content' answer the questions" (McTighe & Wiggins, 2004, p. 106).

Again, the issue of quantity might arise. What number of essential questions is reasonable for a course? Wiggins and McTighe recommend about two to five questions per unit (McTighe & Wiggins, 2004, p. 121); their units relate to the primary or secondary classroom. Translated to the college environment, addressing one or two such questions per week might be sufficient and provides a helpful way of sequencing course activities throughout the semester.

Topical vs. Overarching, and Open vs. Guiding Questions

We need to make one more distinction regarding essential questions, that between "overarching" and "topical" questions. These are matters of scope. The overarching questions are particularly well-suited for framing programs of study, thus holding together whole sets of courses. Topical questions stimulate thinking in a given course with its limited frame of reference. Some examples from McTighe and Wiggins (2004, p. 92) are shown in figure 5.3.

McTighe and Wiggins suggest that effective courses will use related sets of such questions, occasionally moving back and forth between the topical and overarching question. The former raises an issue in the limited context of a single unit or a single course; the latter extends the issue to a broader

FIGURE 5.3
Overarching vs. Topical Questions

Overarching Questions	Topical Questions
Art: *In what ways does art reflect culture as well as shape it?*	Unit or course on masks: *What do masks and their use reveal about the culture?*
Literature: *How do effective writers hook and hold their readers?*	Course on mysteries: *How do great mystery writers hook and hold their readers?*
Science: *How does an organism's structure enable it to survive in its environment?*	Unit on insects: *How do the structure and behavior of insects enable them to survive?*
History/Government: *How do governments balance the rights of individuals with the common good?*	Unit on the U.S. Constitution: *In what ways does the Constitution attempt to limit abuse of government powers?*

(McTighe and Wiggins, 2004)

scale suited for the program level and for discussing issues of theoretical importance to the discipline as a whole.

Guiding Concepts

How Guiding Concepts Subsume Course Topics

Because the purpose of essential questions is to foster conceptual understanding, course design has to identify the key concepts that need to be addressed in trying to answer those questions. Figure 5.4 provides an example that illustrates the connection between understandings and concepts. Again, we start with enduring understandings as the broadest base for our essential questions. The issues raised by those questions are then addressed by sets of discipline-specific concepts. Those concepts are selected for their appropriateness to the course level and competencies of the students.

Erickson (2002) gives a definition of a concept and lists its attributes: "A concept is an organizing idea; a mental construct." Its attributes include:

FIGURE 5.4
From Enduring Understandings to Essential Questions and Key Concepts
PSYCHOLOGY

Enduring Understandings	Essential Questions	Guiding Concepts
Research on motivation has moved from grand to mini-theories	1. Do multiple "mini-theories" explain human behavior better than comprehensive attempts at theory-building? 2. What is the difference between a motivational principle and a motivational theory?	*The mini-theories behind the concepts of:* 1. Self-concept 2. Belonging and attachment 3. Curiosity 4. Achievement 5. Ego defenses 6. Arousal
Self-reports (on which parts of motivation theories are based) are susceptible to errors	1. Can we observe the causes of our actions directly? 2. Where are introspections deceiving? (see attribution theory) 3. What motivates you, and how is that similar or different from what motivates others?	1. Introspection 2. Attribution and schema 3. Causality 4. Correlation 5. Multiple realities 6. Logical fallacies

- Timelessness
- Universality
- Abstractness and breadth
- Represented by 1 or 2 words
- Examples sharing common attributes (p. 56)

Their relative timelessness makes concepts particularly well-suited to organizing the ever-changing and expanding knowledge base that every discipline generates. Whereas the factual knowledge of a discipline tends to shift constantly, concepts tend to remain more stable and are applicable to an increasing number of exemplars. This constitutes another benefit that concepts contribute to course and curriculum design. Important concepts can and should be used over and over again as students move through their courses. As they are applied to a changing list of topics, they gain increasing definition and complexity, because learners see new connections as they move through their academic programs. It is an inductive process that increases students' sophistication about how their discipline is organized and how new knowledge is produced. The instructors' goal is to facilitate transfer of knowledge. To accomplish this, they have to carefully determine for themselves—prior to instruction—on which key concepts they want their students to focus in class.

Macro- vs. Micro-Concepts: Breadth vs. Depth of Understanding

Earlier, we pointed out the distinction between "overarching" and "topical" essential questions. Guiding concepts also differ in size between macro- and micro-concepts. Macro-concepts are larger and more integrating because they apply to many contexts and often cut across multiple disciplines: patterns, systems, structures, cycles, and function are examples. For instance, "patterns" is an important concept, not only in the visual arts, but also in music, literature, even mathematics. The macro-concept "form" applies to music ("musical form"), to art (as "style"), to language arts (as "literary genre"), and to science (as "life-form" or "species"). Erickson (2002, 2007) and Carol Tomlinson and others (2002) provide many more examples.

Micro-concepts are narrower in scope (e.g., most of the psychology concepts in figure 5.4). I have noticed that it can be a challenge to get the faculty of a given department to agree on a list of only fifteen to twenty-five key concepts for a specific course. But there is little doubt that, given enough time and collaborative spirit, most representatives from any discipline could come up with a short list of key concepts that (almost) everyone in their field would consider crucial for their students to understand.

Whereas macro-concepts provide breadth of understanding, micro-concepts deliver depth (Erickson, 2007). As with overarching vs. topical questions, it is probably most useful if instructors plan for the interplay of micro- and macro-concepts. Both allow the integration of content over multiple courses, but macro-concepts in particular also allow for interdisciplinary connections that help students look beyond their own fields for a broader understanding of the subject of their studies.

Course Content and Critical Thinking

How They Are Connected

I summarize the key elements for course content in figure 5.5. It illustrates the close relationship of essential questions and guiding concepts not only

FIGURE 5.5
PY-624: Theories of Motivation

Enduring Understandings	Common Misconceptions	Essential Questions	Guiding Concepts
Behavior is influenced by *external* incentives and *internal* needs.	1. Rewards are good. 2. Successful people are good at setting goals for themselves. 3. Self-esteem is built through other people's praise.	1. How can rewards undermine motivation? 2. Is goal-setting enough to increase achievement? 3. How can low self-esteem be changed?	1. Extrinsic motivation 2. Intrinsic motivation 3. Perceived locus of control 4. Reward and punishment 5. Optimal challenge 6. Achievement motivation 7. Goal setting 8. Self-efficacy 9. Learned helplessness
Motivation involves the interaction of *emotion* and *cognition*.	1. Behavior is either determined by emotion or cognition. 2. Defense mechanisms are bad.	1. Can emotions (e.g., anger) be controlled by cognitions? 2. How does what we think influence what we feel? 3. Do we need to create a false sense of reality to maintain our "sanity"?	1. Attribution errors 2. Ego defenses 3. Self-concept 4. Cognitive dissonance 5. Learned helplessness 6. Perceived locus of control
Motivation varies in *intensity* and *type*.	1. Studying (in school) is boring. 2. Stress is bad. 3. Competition is good.	1. Why do so many young people seem "bored" with school? 2. Which experiences are "stressful"? 3. Is risk-taking necessary for feeling alive?	1. Temperament 2. Optimal arousal 3. Homeostasis 4. Sensation seeking 5. Extraversion vs. introversion
Motivation varies *across* people from different *cultural backgrounds*.	1. We all have the same psychological needs. 2. Key values are universal (e.g., individualism, achievement, competition, self-actualization). 3. Children need both parents to grow into healthy adults.	1. Why do different people develop different explanations (optimism vs. pessimism) for what happens to them? 2. Why do people in some cultures develop a higher need for achievement than people in other cultures? 3. Are attachment patterns different across cultures?	1. Values 2. Individualism vs. collectivism 3. Competition vs. collaboration 4. Work ethic 5. Culture 6. Optimism vs. pessimism

with enduring understandings but also, in many cases, with the false beliefs that students bring to the classroom. This establishes the connection with critical thinking, as described in the previous chapter.

Each enduring understanding is threatened by a number of false beliefs that students tend to bring to the discipline (column two). Most of these false beliefs should be addressed by one of the essential questions in column three, which in turn are linked to the guiding concepts in the fourth column.

For example, the first enduring understanding in figure 5.5 distinguishes between external and internal factors that influence behavior. A common belief, not only of undergraduate students, is that rewards (external incentives for behavior) are a good thing. One of the essential questions for a Theories of Motivation course to raise is, therefore, whether (and how) rewards can actually undermine a person's motivation for autonomous actions. Guiding concepts such as extrinsic vs. intrinsic motivation, perceived locus of control, and self-efficacy play an important role in the conceptual understanding of this issue.

This illustrates how properly selected course content (in the form of essential questions and guiding concepts) can not only address the enduring understandings and learning outcomes of the course but also the comprehension barriers that students face in that course. Not all essential questions are phrased to address students' false beliefs, but they provide a helpful tool for focusing students' attention as they move through the course.

EDUCATIVE ASSESSMENT

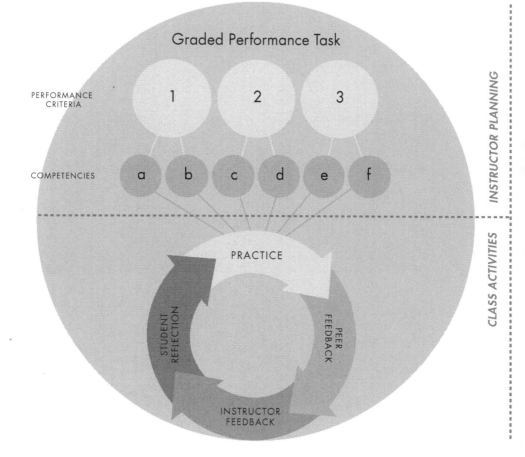

6

ASSESSMENT, PART 1:
EDUCATIVE ASSESSMENT

OVERVIEW

ASSESSMENT FOR GRADING

- Historical reasons for outdated notions of assessment
- Why these notions are no longer useful

ASSESSMENT FOR LEARNING

- Four types of barriers for understanding
- Why authentic performance tasks are essential
- Examples of authentic performance tasks

A CONTINUUM OF ASSESSMENTS

- How to think like an assessor
- Different types and levels of assessment evidence

ASSESSMENT AS COACHING

- Why students need room for making mistakes
- The importance of self-assessment and self-adjustment
- Embedding skills practice into performance tasks

PRINCIPLES OF ASSESSING FOR UNDERSTANDING

- Eight principles for meaningful assessment

ıly way we can properly judge where we
are is relative to where we want to be."
                           —Grant Wiggins, 1998, p. 1

Like the content chapter, the assessment chapter, too, is divided into
two separate parts. The first part will talk about assessment from a
learning-theoretical perspective, and the second part focuses more
on the practical tasks that help us evaluate the quality of the work our
students do.

Assessment for Grading

Historical Reasons for Outdated Notions of Assessment

In a chapter entitled "How American Education Got Into the Testing Trap,"
Ruth Mitchell (1992) outlined the history that led us into an assessment
dilemma affecting the whole U.S. education system: primary, secondary, and
postsecondary. American education started as a two-track system, with private
schools for the elite and a factory model of public schooling designed to
provide workers for a mass-production economy. The latter was based on
the assembly line, which made for simplicity and efficiency. Soon, Tayloristic
production models were matched by behavioristic learning theories. Both
broke (manufacturing or learning) tasks into small steps that were sequenced
for incremental assembly. For decades, these processes were thought to opti-
mize labor or learning productivity, respectively. Behaviorism measured student progress by acquisition of often minute knowledge bits. Schools rewarded
successful acquisition of isolated facts and resorted to student-tracking if differences in performance suggested different ability levels in learners. Frequent
assessment and testing became the hallmark of behavioristic schooling, with
multiple-choice testing being the quintessential tool for probing into context-
free learning that made little reference to meaningful application.

Why These Notions Are No Longer Useful

Some of that tradition still lingers on. Stiehl and Lewchuk (2008, p. 50)
continue to see, throughout our education systems, a "measurement mania,"
with a host of negative consequences for student learning and deep understanding. This ongoing trend of formalizing and standardizing assessment
for the sake of "hard evidence" and "accountability" creates a coercive environment, in which the push for uniformity eliminates experimentation and

discovery. Students become disengaged and lose their natural excitement for learning something new. Competition rules student-to-student interactions. And assessment is separated from the actual learning experience and turns into something threatening rather than helpful.

Similarly, Wiggins deplores the simplistic nature of objective testing that most often seems designed to assess what is easy to test rather than to go after the complex skills (such as critical thinking and lifelong learning) that faculty intend to teach in their courses. "We sacrifice information about what we truly want to assess and settle for score accuracy and efficiency" (Wiggins, 1998, p. 7). Wiggins's analogy: Would you feel safe in a state where people can get a driver's license simply by doing well on a paper-and-pencil test? Passing students in school or college on the regurgitation of book knowledge is the equivalent of the department of motor vehicles deciding that drivers' education should involve extensive book work and tests of driving strategy because actual road tests are simply not worth the hassle, and the tester's judgment during the driving test would be too subjective to hold up under scrutiny.

Assessment should focus less on the reliability of student grades and the speediness with which those grades can be assigned, and concentrate more on capturing what is really worth learning, such as driving a car safely toward one's destination. In order to accomplish that, assessment cannot be a detached act that occurs after teaching has ended, but needs to accompany the learning process when students are still open to corrective actions.

Assessment for Learning

Four Types of Barriers for Understanding

Assessment for learning does not just look at inert knowledge or skills. It investigates where students are in their process of uncovering knowledge and making it their own. But this effort toward understanding is a journey that is characterized by all kinds of mishaps. Chapter 4 described four categories of barriers to critical thinking, and there are likely more than these four that we are currently aware of. Each of these presents its peculiar challenges to student learning, putting a particular lens on the way students look at things that clouds their understanding and their study behaviors. The categories described in chapter 4 illustrate the complex nature of (not!) understanding that is rarely considered in course design and therefore tends to escape assessment procedures. And yet, trying to assess students' level of understanding without addressing these systematic barriers to their understanding really misses the point. Student learning is threatened by at least these four factors:

- Their level of intellectual development, which is characterized by rather distinct (and often simplistic) views of what constitutes knowledge, truth, and subject-matter authority.
- An affective disposition that prejudges the views of others along two dimensions: "favorable" (agrees with me) and "unfavorable" (disagrees with me). To overcome this self-centered perception of the world, a number of "habits of mind," such as intellectual humility and integrity, that allow more realistic evaluations of what one encounters, must be developed.
- Misconceptions based on early experiences and naive theories that preclude acceptance of new and more sophisticated concepts and theories taught in academic disciplines.
- Fallacies of informal reasoning that impede logical discourse because learners have not mastered the intricacies of a complex argument. They might fail to recognize the underlying issue, accept insufficient evidence, jump to conclusions, or miss important implications.

Therefore, students must first be helped to "unlearn" deep-rooted beliefs, attitudes, and misunderstandings before being able to benefit from what an academic discipline has to offer. Concentrating on learning that makes inroads into preexisting layers of intellectual "undergrowth" opens up new tasks for assessment that the traditional knowledge-acquisition view of learning completely ignores. The latter is merely product-oriented, whereas the former is equally concerned with process.

Why Authentic Performance Tasks Are Essential

How can we best assess such learning? Objective tests, especially of the multiple-choice type, are not suited to find out what students misunderstand or which preconceptions are getting in the way of their full comprehension. As long as the instructor does not know exactly where the stumbling blocks lie, he or she will not be able to create a systematic testing procedure to identify the students' difficulties. The only way to assess students' depth of understanding is to have them perform a task that is identical or similar to what a practitioner in the field has to do when solving a problem, facing a difficult situation, or creating a complex product.

Besides, it can be argued that in-depth understanding of complex ideas requires applying those ideas in realistic contexts. After all, professionals in any field acquire competency, not merely by hearing or reading about their field, but by "doing" their field. If students are to really understand their discipline's ideas, they need to perform tasks with them. That represents another principle of idea-based learning. To help instructors create such "authentic performance tasks," Wiggins (1998, pp. 22–24) lists the following criteria:

1. Be realistically contextualized:
   It has situational characteristics and constraints that test a person's abilities to transfer theoretical knowledge to a real-world context. Everyday situations are complex and rarely provide only the limited information that a person needs to solve a problem.
2. Require judgment and innovation:
   In real life, the situation that creates a problem tends to be more complex than the scenarios described in textbooks. Therefore, learners are challenged to figure out for themselves what the actual problem is and what knowledge and skills they must bring to bear in order to address it.
3. Ask the student to "do" the subject:
   Rather than just talking about a problem, learners are required to apply what they know and do the type of work, maybe in a realistic simulation, that would be required in the field.
4. Replicate key challenging situations in which professionals are truly "tested" in the workplace or in their personal life:
   Following point #1, realistic contexts tend to be "messy," impose constraints, and contain distracting variables. Real professionals have to feel their way through such situations, consult a variety of people, change their perception of the problem, and seek feedback throughout the problem-solving process.
5. Assess the student's ability to use a repertoire of knowledge and skill:
   A complex, multistage task requires a problem-solver to make use of integrated knowledge, skill, and feedback that go beyond what a student has learned in the most recent chapter discussed in class.
6. Allow appropriate opportunities to rehearse, practice, and get feedback:
   Formative feedback is an important teaching and learning tool. Traditional course assignments emphasize the need to judge students' work and assign a grade. Authentic performance tasks are designed to be part of the learning act itself, which uses feedback to help the student learn from mistakes and improve performance.

Examples of Authentic Performance Tasks

Here are some short sketches of examples of authentic performance tasks from a variety of disciplines, as provided by several authors. They illustrate what Huba and Freed (2000) have called the "ill-defined" nature of real-life problems that "require judgment, planning, the use of strategies, and the implementation of previously learned skill repertoires."

Mathematics

Design a game that you know you will win (in the long run). Convince us by using combinatorics, probability, and the expectation that you are guaranteed to win. Your game should be easy to describe to potential players, and the outcome of the game should be ambiguous at first glance, or should seem like the other players will win. (McTighe & Wiggins, 2004, p. 33)

Geography

You are an intern at the Regional Office of Tourism that has been asked to prepare a four-day trip for a group of nine foreign visitors (who speak English). Plan the tour, including a budget, so that the visitors are shown sites that help them understand the key historic, geographic, and economic features of our region. Explain why each site was selected and how it will help the visitors understand those important features of our region. (McTighe & Wiggins, 2004, p. 171)

History

President Harry S. Truman has requested that you serve on a White House task force. The goal is to decide how to force the unconditional surrender of Japan, yet provide for a secure postwar world. (Huba & Freed, 2000, p. 204)

You are members of Lyndon B. Johnson's Kerner Commission, which is to determine the causes of urban rioting in the '60s. The Commission is to develop a report on why the violence erupted and what can be done about it. The report must be thoughtful and thorough, and it will be presented to the President and the country. (McTighe & Wiggins, 2004, p. 44)

Chemistry

You are a researcher hired by a group of expert mountain climbers. Hypoxia is the set of symptoms (headache, fatigue, nausea) that comes from a lack of oxygen in body tissues. It is often felt by mountain climbers as they ascend altitude quickly. Sherpas, longtime residents of high altitudes, seem to feel no hypoxic discomfort. Why might that be? Your group wants to know and benefit from the knowledge. Design a series of experiments that would test the difference in hypoxic symptoms between mountain climbers and Sherpas. Explain, using chemical equilibrium, why high altitude causes hypoxia in the climbers. How can Sherpas avoid these symptoms? How can you test for these possibilities?

What would a positive test look like? What inherent errors would you have to be aware of? (McTighe & Wiggins, 2004, p. 168)

Psychology
- *Design a behavioral intervention for the out-of-seat behavior of a student with ADD.*
- *Develop and execute a behavior-modification program for an "addiction" (overeating, drinking too much soda pop, watching too much TV, etc.) that you yourself struggle with.*
- *Develop and conduct a small research study that compares consumers' preferences for a particular product.*
- *Analyze a work environment, e.g., a campus department's front office, and propose improvements in work procedures (IO-Psych).*
- *Do some volunteer work at a retirement home and prepare an informal, unobtrusive assessment of the mental health of the people who live there.*

A final example comes from the Theories of Motivation course and illustrates how the performance tasks connect with the learning outcomes of the course (see figure 6.1).

The first four learning outcomes can be assessed at least partially with performance task #1, in which students are asked to reflect and write, over a period of time, about their own behavior as it relates to intellectual curiosity, achievement motivation, and self-concept. As long as the instructor explicitly links the performance task to these four learning outcomes of the course, the reflective writing allows insight into the students' understanding of what impacts their own daily experiences and the mechanisms for turning these experiences into personal preferences.

Performance task #2 allows students to both increase and demonstrate their understanding of some of the same learning outcomes by conducting a real psychological study that requires inquiry methods for gaining insight into other people's behavior. This is the task that is most similar to what real professionals do in the field.

Performance task #3 is similar to the first performance task in that it requires more reflection on what students themselves have done, but this reflection is now related to the research procedures that the students performed in task #2. It thereby allows students to think about the theoretical concepts of the course while applying them to a real-world scenario. As they reflect critically on how helpful these concepts have been in analyzing their research-subjects' behaviors, students also reveal how well they have or have not understood those concepts.

FIGURE 6.1
Outcomes and Related Performance Tasks

Related Outcomes Students become aware of:	Performance Task
1: Reasons for own behavior. 2: How cognitive mechanisms overcome motivational tendencies. 3: Reasons for seeking or avoiding experiences. 4: Individual differences within cultural contexts.	TASK 1: Keep a reflective journal about a personal behavior that indicates lack of curiosity, desire to achieve, or low self-concept.
2: How cognitive mechanisms overcome motivational tendencies. 3: Reasons for seeking or avoiding experiences. 4: Individual differences within cultural contexts. 5. Implications of different motivation theories.	TASK 2: Develop and conduct a research project (in the new tradition of Positive Psychology) that investigates a population exhibiting positive behavior, lifestyle, and/or mind-set regarding one of the six types of motivation.
5. Implications of different motivation theories. 6. Compatibility and contradiction of theories. 7. Shortcomings of introspection.	TASK 3: Analyze the strengths and weaknesses of your research project and describe them in a short essay.

A Continuum of Assessments

How to Think Like an Assessor

Assessment in an outcomes-based framework is not primarily intended for grading. Its purpose is to define what types of evidence might be sufficient to convince the instructor that the student has truly understood the course concepts and is able to use the skills taught. Wiggins and McTighe (2005) call on the instructor to "think like an assessor" when designing learning outcomes and related instructional activities. To drive home their point, they draw on the legal profession with its dictum: "innocent (of understanding, skill, and so on) until proven guilty by a preponderance of evidence that is more than circumstantial" (p. 148). They then lay out three basic questions the instructor-assessor needs to ask:

1. What *kinds of evidence* do we need to find hallmarks of our goals, including that of understanding?
2. What specific *characteristics in student responses*, products, or performances should we examine to determine the extent to which the desired results were achieved?
3. Does the proposed evidence *enable us to infer* a student's knowledge, skills, or understanding? (p. 150)

Different Types and Levels of Assessment Evidence

In order to answer these questions, the assessment system in a class needs to involve more than just a few snapshots during the semester. Collecting the type of evidence called for in the above questions requires ongoing investigation. That investigation looks at student products but also at their gradual progress toward achievement of the learning outcomes. To accomplish this, the instructor needs to collect a variety of evidence, ranging from small indicators of localized skill mastery to much more comprehensive documentation of students' overall understanding.

Because of their complex challenges, authentic performance tasks play the key role in such an assessment system. They provide the best indication of the students' ability to independently and creatively apply their knowledge under real or simulated conditions, and thereby document the full degree of their understanding. Criteria for and examples of such authentic tasks were described previously.

Other indicators of student-learning include open-ended *academic prompts* that, like authentic performance tasks, have no single best answer or use no single correct problem-solving strategy. They require students to think critically and explain or defend their answer, but tend to be less than "authentic," because their context is limited in scope and serves mainly to practice a new skill.

Quizzes and test items also remain useful for assessing simple content knowledge that is relevant for performing the more complex tasks already mentioned. These formats typically expect selection of a single correct or best answer and can be easily and quickly scored to provide fast feedback.

Finally, there is a host of *informal checks* that take place on a daily basis but don't usually receive a grade. They may include simple observations of students' brainstorming or problem solving in small groups, one-on-one interactions with a student working quietly on a task, classroom assessment activities like the ones promoted by Thomas Angelo and Patricia Cross (1993), or instructor feedback on drafts of paper assignments.

All this constitutes a continuum of assessments (Wiggins & McTighe, 2005) designed to provide an ongoing audit trail of student growth and learning in the course. With assessment being ongoing, it appears that teaching and assessing become virtually identical, because every teaching move is ideally based on an assessment of the students' latest learning progress.

Assessment as Coaching

Why Students Need Room for Making Mistakes

This assessment–teaching symbiosis becomes even more obvious when looking at the role the instructor plays in assessments that are not done for grading purposes, that is, in formative rather than summative assessment. Learning requires practice, and practice of complex tasks always involves trial and error and learning from mistakes. Traditional notions of assessment leave little room for mistakes, which are typically seen as failure to learn. By contrast, assessing for learning makes room for mistakes in the learning process: "Nothing worth understanding is mastered the first time" (Wiggins, 1998, p. 15). Students learn from making errors and receiving feedback that helps them get back on track. Effective feedback is timely, frequent, and usually delivered in a descriptive (rather than a judgmental) language. It is a matter of coaching, in which the student welcomes and expects ongoing feedback to help him or her make progress.

The Importance of Self-Assessment and Self-Adjustment

A key in this process is that students learn to react to feedback by adjusting their performance through repeated practice opportunities. As this repeats itself over many instances, students eventually learn to self-assess and self-adjust. Complex tasks in the real world (such as raising children or developing a financial plan for a business) require adaptive performance. People need to figure out when to pause, reassess, and modify their strategy, based on new information. "Self-adjustment is not something we can leave to chance between tests if our aim is to determine whether students are effective in the use of knowledge and skill" (Wiggins, 1998, p. 61). Students need help in learning how to assess their own progress and to make the necessary adjustments for reaching higher levels of competency. Academic excellence is not possible without the ability to self-assess and self-adjust. (See figure 6.2 for practical suggestions for self-assessment tasks.)

FIGURE 6.2
Dimensions of Reflection and Self-Assessment

Self-assessment and reflection are key components to becoming a critical thinker. Students need to be given opportunities to reflect about the quality of their own (and others') learning in order to improve their thinking skills. Every course provides a variety of opportunities for such activities. The following is a brief selection.

1. **Assessing Others**
   a. Peer feedback on others' writing drafts
   b. Peer feedback on oral presentations, using a scoring rubric
   c. Peer feedback on others' contributions to group work
   d. Feedback on the instructor's conducting of the course

2. **Assessing Own Performance**
   a. Assessment of own writing, using rubrics
   b. Reflection on peer feedback received from others

3. **Assessing Self in Group Activities**
   a. Written reflections on one's own contribution to the group process
   b. Written reflections on what one learned from the group work

4. **Assessing Own Learning Progress**
   a. Reflection on comprehension of lectures
   b. Reflection on what was learned in a whole course
   c. Reflection on a whole course of studies

5. **Assessing Own Goals and Interests**
   a. Reflection/discussion about choosing a major (e.g., in office hour)
   b. Reflection on what the student expects from a course
   c. Goal analysis based on assessment of own strengths and weaknesses (e.g., through learning style inventory)

Embedding Skills Practice Into Performance Tasks

As crucial as authentic performances are to assessing the depth of their understanding, students also need opportunities to practice simpler component skills. Sports coaches do simple sideline drills to prepare their players for a game. Similarly, college students need "sideline drills" (Wiggins, 1998, p. 36) to develop isolated skill sets and bodies of knowledge that provide the basis for complex, authentic tasks later on. Students need safe environments to practice the component skills relevant for real-life performance.

By contrast, traditional "assembly-line" instruction has focused on details at the expense of the larger picture that gives meaning to the details. Coaches have their teams do sideline drills to get ready for the next game, not as a means to grade the performance of their players. This approach is very different from the attitude frequently displayed in lower-level courses, which is based on the assumption that students first need to learn "the basics" before (in the upper-level courses) they are to apply this basic knowledge in meaningful contexts.

There is a wealth of examples for interactive classroom techniques that provide students with the necessary practice opportunities for various types of competencies. For example, Elizabeth Barkley, in her book *Student Engagement Techniques* (2010), lists fifty such techniques that address both course-related knowledge and skills as well as techniques for developing learner attitudes, values, and self-awareness. Similarly, chapter 10 in this volume describes a number of technology-mediated approaches to help students practice anything from basic skills to complex inquiry tasks.

Principles of Assessing for Understanding

Eight Principles for Meaningful Assessment

Assessment for understanding requires careful planning and a variety of assessment approaches. As important as variety is in the types of evidence that the instructor collects, equally if not more important is that true understanding ultimately reveals itself in performance that is embedded in rich, authentic contexts. The complexity of those contexts challenges students to demonstrate how well they can transfer the knowledge, skills, and core ideas they have learned in the course. With that in mind, Wiggins (1998) described 14 implications for assessing understanding, of which I am listing those that, in my view, are the most important ones:

- Use simulations or real applications that require students to use knowledge with a purpose and a context in mind. (p. 96)
- Design interactive assessments. We need to know why students have done what they have done. (p. 91)
- Use reiterative core-performance tasks to determine if understanding is becoming more sophisticated over time. (p. 91)
- In light of the inevitability of misconception, use assessment tasks that will best evoke such misunderstandings. (p. 92)

- Design curricula and build tests around recurring essential questions that give rise to important theories and stories, and challenge students to look for the big picture. (p. 94)
- Use rubrics that measure the degree of sufficiency and the power of the answers, not simply their correctness. (p. 97)
- Require students to self-assess their previous as well as their present work in order to gain insight into how sophisticated and accurate a student's view is of the tasks, criteria, and standards that he or she is to master. (p. 92)
- Assess student self-adjustment in response to human or situational feedback. (p. 96)

RUBRICS IN ASSESSMENT

QUALITY CRITERIA	NO/LIMITED PROFICIENCY	SOME PROFICIENCY	PROFICIENCY	HIGH PROFICIENCY
CRITERION #1	Description of what a performance of no or limited proficiency on CRITERION #1 would look like	Description of what a performance of some proficiency on CRITERION #1 would look like	Description of what a performance of proficiency on CRITERION #1 would look like	Description of what a performance of high proficiency on CRITERION #1 would look like
CRITERION #2	Description of what a performance of no or limited proficiency on CRITERION #2 would look like	Description of what a performance of some proficiency on CRITERION #2 would look like	Description of what a performance of proficiency on CRITERION #2 would look like	Description of what a performance of high proficiency on CRITERION #2 would look like
CRITERION #3	Description of what a performance of no or limited proficiency on CRITERION #3 would look like	Description of what a performance of some proficiency on CRITERION #3 would look like	Description of what a performance of proficiency on CRITERION #3 would look like	Description of what a performance of high proficiency on CRITERION #3 would look like
CRITERION #4	Description of what a performance of no or limited proficiency on CRITERION #4 would look like	Description of what a performance of some proficiency on CRITERION #4 would look like	Description of what a performance of proficiency on CRITERION #4 would look like	Description of what a performance of high proficiency on CRITERION #4 would look like
CRITERION #5	Description of what a performance of no or limited proficiency on CRITERION #5 would look like	Description of what a performance of some proficiency on CRITERION #5 would look like	Description of what a performance of proficiency on CRITERION #5 would look like	Description of what a performance of high proficiency on CRITERION #5 would look like
CRITERION #6	Description of what a performance of no or limited proficiency on CRITERION #6 would look like	Description of what a performance of some proficiency on CRITERION #6 would look like	Description of what a performance of proficiency on CRITERION #6 would look like	Description of what a performance of high proficiency on CRITERION #6 would look like

7

ASSESSMENT, PART 2: RUBRICS

OVERVIEW

EXAMPLES OF ASSIGNMENTS LACKING CLEAR CRITERIA

THE MAIN PARTS OF A RUBRIC

- Dimensions of quality
- Levels of mastery (scale)
- Commentaries (description of dimensions)

COMMON MISUNDERSTANDINGS ABOUT RUBRICS

- "Rubrics are just for program assessment"
- "Rubrics are only for the eyes of the instructor"
- "Rubrics are just for grading student assignments"
- "Rubrics restrict creative thinking"
- "Rubrics present an information overload"

THE TRIPLE FUNCTION OF RUBRICS

- Instructor assessment of students
- Student self-assessment: Rubrics as teaching tools
- Program assessment

Examples of Assignments Lacking Clear Criteria

Outcomes-based instruction needs to align the intended learning outcomes with the assessment of what students actually accomplish in the course. That is not an easy task and requires the means to translate broader learning outcomes into very specific performances. Too often, vague relationships between initially declared outcomes and assignments given later in the course are postulated but never clearly established.

The next few paragraphs display the instructions for completing key assignments in General Education courses some 10 years ago. Consider the ambiguity and lack of detail in the following anonymous syllabus that make it difficult, if not impossible, for students to figure out exactly what the instructors are asking them to do and how their performances will be evaluated.

> *Music:*
>
> Write a research paper. There are several options for this paper. You may choose your own topic but it must be approved by the instructor. Here are some suggestions:
>
> - Outline the history of a specific instrument or musical genre.
> - Outline the musical history of a specific country, state, or region.
> - Compare the musical works of several composers in the same genre.
> - Provide a study of European musicians who traveled to America.
>
> The research paper must be at least three full pages, typed, double-spaced. It is mandatory to use *The New Grove Dictionary of Music and Musicians.* Include a bibliography and/or footnotes citing this and any other materials that you consulted.
>
> Beware of solely relying on data from the Internet and some CD ROMs. These may offer good initial ideas but it is preferable to use *The New Grove Dictionary* and several books devoted to your topic.

This assignment provides two types of information: the kinds of topics the instructor desires for this paper, and the format for the paper, including acceptable reference sources. The overall focus is clearly on content, with no indication of the quality criteria for addressing this content. This seems even more problematic when one considers the broad and potentially intimidating scale of these topics, combined with the fact that they are to be dealt with in the space of three double-spaced pages. What types of learning outcomes could possibly be addressed with such an assignment?

Women's Studies/Cultural Studies:

A final 5–7 page paper will be due the last day of class. It can be on a topic of your choice related to themes of the class, provided you obtain my approval for your topic at least three weeks prior to its due date. Otherwise, I will assign a topic. It will be based on our readings, discussions, the workshops—everything we do in the class. This paper is to be typed. I will ask each of you on the last day of class to give a short 5 to 10 minute presentation to the class on what you write about.

The instructor apparently wants to provide maximum opportunity for students to write about what has been most relevant and interesting for them in the course. Every part of the course materials is fair game; there are no restrictions, although the instructor builds in one "safety," that is prior instructor approval of the topic. No explicit quality criteria are given in the instructions. Students will have to take the plunge and, inspired by the instructor's teaching approach exhibited throughout the course, infer what criteria might be appropriate for writing such a paper. Many students, who were used to considerable structure in their high school years, might not be able to do this in the early semesters of their college education.

Sociology:

You will submit a series of seven Response Papers (2–3 pages each) of your reactions to our films, readings, lectures, and classroom discussions. This assignment will allow you to react individually to our common classroom experiences and to write in a more personal style. It will allow your instructor to evaluate each individual's level of engagement with our course materials and our class. Also, *your response papers should provide a basis for your participation in class discussions.*

Your Response Papers will be scored on a fraction scale from 5/10 (lowest possible score) to 10/10 (highest possible score). These papers will also be measured against other student papers turned in during a given week with regard to the following factors:

- Completeness of thoughts
- Quality of ideas
- Grammatical presentation
- How well the student essay weaves a web that thoughtfully integrates ideas from the written texts, film texts, in-class discussions, and her/his own lived experiences

Response papers have become a popular format for regularly engaging students with the content of the class. Besides fostering frequent active engagement with the content, their objective tends to be, as in the above case, to encourage "writing-to-learn," which allows for a more personal writing style than a formal term paper would require. The instructor wants to pursue a dual goal with this assignment: to have students do some explicit thinking on paper and to thereby get them ready to participate in class discussions. The instructor also spells out some criteria for assessing the student papers, but these criteria remain rather vague. In fact, one wonders whether students might get confused by the two functions of the assignment: to present "completeness of thoughts" while at the same time providing "a basis for . . . in class discussions," which might actually be better served with ("non-complete") questions and tentative objections to course materials. The notion that "papers will also be measured against other student papers" might ultimately defeat the purpose of providing criteria of quality as the reliable measuring stick for student work.

The Main Parts of a Rubric

The sample assignments presented fail to clearly convey instructor expectations or how the assignments are related to the course's learning outcomes. Even if the instructors had links in mind between assignments and course outcomes, those links were not evident. These problems with course assignments occur as long as instructors do not identify the criteria by which to judge quality work that is aligned with the course outcomes. One of the most useful ways to help students understand instructor expectations is to create a grading rubric. Rubrics clarify both for the instructor and the students what the ultimate objectives are for an assignment. They do this by defining the following three major elements:

Dimensions of Quality

The left-hand column in figure 7.1 illustrates the quality criteria one might apply to a complex critical-thinking task, such as a term paper that requires students to analyze a problem scenario in their discipline. This particular rubric was created (by Northeastern Illinois University's General Education Committee and is based on Washington State's critical-thinking rubric) to assess critical-thinking skills across a variety of General Education courses. Its quality criteria are therefore fairly generic and not geared toward any particular assignment. The six criteria selected are gleaned from theories of critical thinking and represent what most of them would consider to be

FIGURE 7.1
NEIU's Critical Thinking Rubric

Quality / Criteria	No/Limited Proficiency (0–1 points)	Some Proficiency (2 points)	Proficiency (3 points)	High Proficiency (4 points)	Rating (1,2,3,4pts.)
1. Identifies and explains ISSUES	Fails to identify, summarize, or explain the main issue. (AND/OR) Represents the issues inaccurately or inappropriately.	Identifies main issues but does not summarize or explain them clearly or sufficiently.	Identifies, summarizes, and briefly explains the main issues, but fails to mention any implicit issues.	Clearly identifies, summarizes, and explains main issues and identifies embedded or implicit issues, addressing their relationships to each other.	
2. Recognizes stakeholders and CONTEXTS (i.e., cultural/social, educational, technological, political, scientific, economic, ethical, personal experience)	Fails to accurately identify and explain any empirical or theoretical contexts for the issues. (OR) Presents problems as having no connections to other conditions or contexts.	Shows some general understanding of the influences of empirical and theoretical contexts on stakeholders, but does not identify any specific ones.	Correctly identifies the empirical and most theoretical contexts relevant to the main stakeholders.	Correctly identifies the empirical and theoretical contexts relevant to the main stakeholders and identifies minor stakeholders and contexts showing the tensions or conflicts of interest among them.	
3. Frames personal responses and acknowledges other PERSPECTIVES	Fails to formulate a personal point of view and fails to consider other perspectives.	Formulates a vague personal point of view and/or vague alternative points of view.	Formulates a clear personal point of view and considers some other perspectives.	Formulates a clear personal point of view and addresses relevant perspectives successfully.	
4. Identifies and evaluates ASSUMPTIONS	Fails to identify and evaluate any of the important assumptions behind the claims and recommendations made.	Identifies some of the most important assumptions, but does not evaluate them for plausibility or clarity.	Identifies and briefly evaluates the important assumptions.	Identifies and carefully evaluates the important assumptions.	
5. Identifies and evaluates EVIDENCE	Fails to correctly identify data and information that counts as evidence for truth-claims (AND/OR) fails to evaluate its credibility.	Correctly identifies data and information that counts as evidence but fails to highlight its relative importance and/or link them with theoretical concepts and frameworks.	Correctly identifies important evidence, highlights its relative importance, and makes an attempt at linking evidence to theoretical concepts and frameworks.	Correctly identifies and rigorously evaluates important evidence, successfully linking the evidence to theoretical concepts and frameworks while providing new or alternative data or information for consideration.	
6. Identifies and evaluates IMPLICATIONS ("What does this mean?")	Fails to identify implications, conclusions, or consequences of the issue.	Suggests some implications, conclusions, or consequences of the issue.	Identifies and briefly evaluates many implications, conclusions, or consequences of the issue.	Identifies and thoroughly evaluates implications, conclusions, or consequences of the issue.	

important critical-thinking characteristics. Assignments in a specific course might focus on some of these and add others that address unique features of the course assignment. (See criteria for the second assignment of my PY-624 course in figure 7.2.) In any case, rubrics have to strike a balance between breaking quality expectations into a number of different criteria and not becoming so complex that students (and faculty) get lost in the subtleties of the distinctions.

Levels of Mastery (Scale)

Each dimension of quality is divided into several (in the case of the Critical Thinking Rubric: four) levels of mastery that create the next columns of figure 7.1. Each mastery level has a label and, typically, also a point value attached. The labels in our rubric are: High Proficiency, Proficiency, Some Proficiency, No/Limited Proficiency. Many other labels are possible and common, for example, Excellent, Good, Needs Improvement, Unaccept-able; or Excellent, Competent, Needs Work, and so on. The number of mastery levels depends on the complexity of the assignment to be assessed. Whereas a complex assignment might require four—in exceptional cases, even five—levels, smaller assignments might sufficiently be judged with just three. The point values attached to each mastery level can be added up, and ranges of total points can be translated into letter grades. Judith Arter and Jay McTighe (2001) prefer a different method for converting scores, using what they call a "logic rule." The logic rule defines how many top scores a student must have on the various criteria, as well as the maximum of lower

FIGURE 7.2
Rubric Criteria for PY-624 Task

TASK 2: *Develop and conduct a research project (in the new tradition of Positive Psychology) that has you investigate a population exhibiting positive behavior, lifestyle, and/or mind-set regarding one of the six types of motivation*

Criteria for this task:

1. Student *identifies appropriate issue* and target population
2. Creates effective research design
3. Collects meaningful data
4. *Analyzes data* based on appropriate psychological concepts
5. *Evaluates relevant implications* of the research

* Criteria 1, 4, and 5 are similar to criteria 1, 5, and 6 in Critical Thinking Rubric

scores tolerated, for the student to receive a particular letter grade on the assignment.

Commentaries (Description of Dimensions)

Now comes the hardest part. Each level of mastery under a given quality criterion is briefly defined with characteristic features that a student product typically shows at that mastery level. For example, in the critical thinking rubric, "high proficiency" in the Evidence criterion is described as *"Correctly identifies and rigorously evaluates important evidence, successfully linking the evidence to theoretical concepts and frameworks . . . ,"* whereas the next lower mastery level ("proficiency") reads, *"Correctly identifies important evidence, highlights its relative importance, and makes an attempt at linking evidence to theoretical concepts and frameworks."* The main difference between the two mastery levels indicates that the merely "proficient" students typically have a harder time linking evidence to theoretical concepts and frameworks, even though they try. The student showing "some proficiency" completely fails in this regard.

What makes these commentaries difficult to write is that they need to be indicative of actual student strengths and weaknesses on the different quality dimensions of the assignment, and they need to qualify, rather than just quantify, the differences in performance. Saying "high proficiency" has 4 characteristics, "proficiency" has 4 minus 1, "some proficiency" has 4 minus 2, and "low proficiency" has 4 minus 3 characteristics rarely captures the actual differences in student work. They need to all be coherent with the given dimension of quality rather than introduce new criteria as they move from high to low proficiency. Finally, they need to be brief enough to be easily scanned within a table and long enough to communicate real performance differences.

The best way to create such commentaries is to take a representative group of student papers and start by sorting them into three or four piles that seem to represent different quality levels, then categorize the common characteristics of each of those piles, and finally condense those characteristics into the commentaries of your rubric. This process guarantees that grading with the rubric is criterion-referenced and does not simply follow a normal curve. You have now not only created dimensions of quality on which to assess student work, but you have also determined for each dimension what the various mastery levels mean and the performance required to reach each of them. By the way, this task does not have to be done exclusively by the instructor. In fact, it tends to be more beneficial when students themselves are involved in developing the rubrics that determine how the quality of their work will be measured. More on this later in the chapter when we look at "rubrics as teaching tools."

My short descriptions of the main features of a rubric are not meant as an exhaustive manual for how to create and apply rubrics in the classroom. This chapter focuses on the functions of rubrics for assessment and for course design in general. For more in-depth treatments of how to build and apply rubrics as a grading tool, consult the growing literature on rubrics in college teaching, especially the respective chapters in Arter and McTighe (2001), Huba and Freed (2000), Stevens and Levi (2005), Suskie (2004), and Wiggins (1998).

Common Misunderstandings About Rubrics

Rubrics have become more common in the college classroom fairly recently. Their rising popularity has been partially because of their usefulness in program assessment. Their application in assessing student work in individual classes has moved at a much slower pace, with some notable exceptions, particularly in colleges of education. Given this relative novelty and the different functions that rubrics can fill, it is not surprising that there are still some misunderstandings surrounding rubrics. Here are some examples.

"Rubrics Are Just for Program Assessment"

In program assessment, a committee usually chooses a rubric to compare student work across classes and course levels within a given program. Such rubrics typically look at how certain student products reflect broad program goals. They do not necessarily capture everything an instructor wants to accomplish with an assignment; they only focus on a few general areas. If faculty have only experienced rubrics in this function, they might not realize the potential for transfer to their individual classroom, because the tool seems too imprecise for measuring the specific objective of their unique class assignment.

"Rubrics Are Only for the Eyes of the Instructor"

The second misunderstanding is related to the previous one. Underlying both is the fear that learning outcomes become too narrow and predictable. Letting students know about the rubric, therefore, is perceived as "teaching to the test." If students are told what the instructor wants to see in a good assignment, then student preparation will narrowly focus on these limited expectations. Accordingly, it is considered a mistake to let students "see" the rubric or to give them practice in understanding and applying its criteria before assigning the work. This misunderstanding relates to the rubric's role; it does not actually tell students which content bits to include in a good assignment, but rather which quality criteria are used to measure what students can do with that content, so that it reveals how well they understand it.

"Rubrics Are Just for Grading Student Assignments"

The idea here is that rubrics are merely a tool to make grading easier for the instructor and, as a side effect, fairer to the students. They are seen as a mnemonic device that helps the instructor remember all the points to consider when grading a student paper, presentation, or other product. As they score multiple papers, instructors tend to tire out and "forget" why they graded earlier papers the way they did. This fatigue effect can lead to subsequently graded papers being judged more leniently or more harshly than those graded earlier. Rubrics counteract this trend and give all students a fairer chance at getting the proper grade. But this narrow view of rubrics overlooks another, possibly even more important function, described in the next segment of this chapter; they are not just a grading tool; they are also a teaching tool.

"Rubrics Restrict Creative Thinking"

A common notion claims that predetermining what would make a good student product (like a term paper) takes the creativity out of student performance. Instructors might think that spelling out ahead of time what they will accept as exceptional work will limit students' imagination, initiative, and sense of responsibility for their own learning. The philosophy behind this seems reasonable; students might never become mature, independent thinkers if they are not challenged to discover for themselves what constitutes good and creative thinking. Giving them the instructor's criteria up front stymies their creativity and puts them in a passive role. This argument overlooks the possibility of involving students in creating a rubric (or rubrics) for the course, integrating the pursuit of creative, unconventional approaches to an assignment as an important assessment criterion, and the potential to gradually phase out rubrics as students progress through college and graduate school and internalize the discipline's criteria for quality work.

"Rubrics Present an Information Overload"

Fully developed rubrics are just too "scary," because of their information density. Seeing a copy of the one-page critical-thinking rubric (figure 7.1) might have that effect on instructors and students alike. But the amount of information packed into this one page (which could also be spread out over multiple pages for easier readability) does not have to be absorbed all at once. A fairly comprehensive rubric such as this one can be broken down into several parts for different assignments. The first course assignment might only address the Issues and Context criteria; a second one might look at Issues, Assumptions, and Evidence; a third one might talk about Perspectives and Implications. Rarely is a complex rubric applied in its entirety to the first course assignment.

The Triple Function of Rubrics

Rubrics have at least three different functions, one each for the instructor, the students, and the program. This is what makes them such an important tool for course and curriculum design. Probably the most important point to remember is that they need to be part of the course-planning process and not an afterthought when the instructor has finalized an assignment. A common problem with many course assignments is that instructors often don't determine what they are (at least not in detail) until the time comes to hand them to the students. The examples at the beginning of this chapter were the complete descriptions of the course assignments as they appeared in those three syllabi. Instructors may work out further details as they approach the due dates, but their exact fit with the course and its learning outcomes is often not part of the course design process itself. Let's review the three functions of rubrics in more detail.

Instructor Assessment of Students

A rubric is a very practical tool that helps with the grading process. Grading complex assignments such as student research papers, oral presentations, and other types of student performances can be difficult and is often considered to be rather subjective, especially by students who are on the receiving side of that process. Complaints are frequent because it is not evident to a student why she received a *B* when her neighbor, who wrote a similar-sized paper with the same amount of references and instructor comments in the margins, received an *A*. Rubrics make this process less subjective. There are distinct dimensions that are evaluated, not the holistic "feel" of the piece, and each dimension is divided into different performance levels, whose characteristics are described in writing. This approach makes complex, qualitative outcomes measurable, so that quantitative points can be assigned. The result is that the grading process is more transparent, consistent, and fair. Instructors using a well-designed rubric find that the number of student complaints about grading goes down almost immediately.

Another practical bonus for the instructor is that rubrics save time with grading. It might take some practice until the instructor has fully internalized the different dimensions and their performance levels, but then the focus on these dimensions allows for faster scanning of the student product. The number of comments in the margins can be significantly reduced because the comments are already in the rubric, where each performance level can be checked and characteristic strengths and weaknesses can be circled. Additional instructor comments are limited to key overall evaluations and suggestions for improvement.

Besides their practical value for grading purposes, rubrics also help the instructor communicate more precisely what he or she wants the students to do. Every instruction contains a certain amount of ambiguity. A rubric reduces this ambiguity by providing concrete indicators of what the instructor intends the students to do. This helps the students, but it also sharpens the instructor's course design. Well-written instructions for a paper can make an assignment sound really interesting and engaging, but they typically lack a clear link to the intended learning outcomes for the course. The detailed criteria of a rubric help align important aspects of an assignment with specific learning outcomes in the course.

Idea-based learning depends on instruction keeping the focus on the main goals. Rubrics are a key tool that helps with this task. The rubric spells out (for instructor and students alike) how the assignment "plugs into" the intended course outcomes. That's why it is important that assignments are fully developed during the course design process and not left vague until shortly before the assignment is handed to the students. If instructors are not fully aware of exactly how they want students to demonstrate their understanding of the course outcomes, then their teaching cannot be clearly focused on these outcomes either.

Student Self-Assessment: Rubrics as Teaching Tools

The second function of rubrics is related to students. Rubrics are the ultimate tool in what was referred to as educative assessment in chapter 6. They communicate to students the instructor's criteria for being successful on a task. They take much of the guessing about the instructor's intentions out of an assignment. Not only can the instructor hold students accountable for their performance, students now have a contract in hand that holds the instructor accountable for the way he or she grades their assignments.

At the same time, a well-written rubric also communicates key criteria of the discipline to the students. Thoughtfully articulated criteria are not idiosyncratic of the instructor; they should reflect the standards in a given field so that students are inducted into the discourse of their field of study. What better place to explain those standards to students than when explaining to them what constitutes quality work! Some of these standards may go beyond individual disciplines and, as in the case of the Critical Thinking Rubric, represent criteria that cut across many fields and are, therefore, reinforced all across a student's General Education courses.

There are also opportunities for students to cooperate with the instructor on the development of a rubric. Stevens and Levi (2005) describe four different models for student involvement that range from reflective class discussion of the criteria set forth in a rubric, to students taking on the main responsibility in creating the rubric. The degree of student involvement depends mainly on the students' academic maturity and the class size. The general rule is that nothing helps with the understanding of criteria as much as being asked to establish those criteria oneself. For example, students who go through the process of reviewing (old) work samples in order to articulate what makes some products better than others develop a unique understanding of what constitutes quality work. The instructor provides appropriate guidance as the students work in small teams to discuss their views before they put them in writing, and the whole class goes through a debriefing phase to compare the rationales that different student teams have developed. As they eventually judge their own work against "their" rubric, they might be given time to revise their first rubric draft. This fosters the recognition that building assessment criteria is a work in progress, that developing judgment is important but is never a finished process.

Idea-based learning is self-reflective and requires students' awareness, not just of the important course concepts, but also of their own progress toward fully understanding them. The overall benefit of rubrics is that knowing the criteria for quality work (whether established by the instructor or co-established by the students) allows for student self-regulation. There is no reason to postpone the assessment of their work to the time the instructor looks at it. Students themselves are called upon to subject their own work to the rubric before submitting it.

By the same token, the rubric allows for substantive peer feedback. Many instructors have been disappointed when asking students to give each other feedback on their papers, seeing that students tended to focus on surface aspects, such as spelling and grammar. Rubrics make peer feedback a doable and rewarding learning activity. The ultimate goal of a college education is to create autonomous learners, people who have developed enough self-awareness that they no longer need the intervention of an instructor who corrects their mistakes and shortcomings. Rubrics are a key tool for helping students become self-corrective in their learning.

Getting students to that point requires considerable coaching. They need to be given ample opportunities and guidance in understanding and practicing what the quality criteria mean and how they are translated into good products. A question guide for what needs to be considered when applying the criteria can be helpful in this regard. Using the Critical Thinking Rubric in this chapter, figure 7.3 illustrates how students can be coached to properly interpret the quality criteria of that rubric. For example, the first criterion asks the student to identify the critical issues and/or questions that are at stake in a given case scenario. Providing the cues "a–e" guides the student's understanding of how to approach the task, for example, rephrasing the question in different ways, breaking it into sub-questions, figuring out whether the question directs the investigation at historical, economic, biological, and so on, issues, or whether the case is about more than just one key question. This helps students as they practice applying the rubric to different cases and learn how it focuses their thinking.

Program Assessment

The third function of rubrics pertains to the coordinated planning and assessment of student learning across courses and over time. Rubrics provide a relatively economical tool for allowing faculty in a department, a program, or even across the whole university to communicate about the skills they want their students to develop. A one- or two-page rubric can be a good indication of what a student should be able to do as a result of having taken a particular course. Short of the full course design document presented in chapter 9, rubrics are a good first tool for a group of faculty to negotiate what a given course should accomplish, how the outcomes of one course prepare a student for taking other courses in the curriculum, and how different courses might best be sequenced so as to maximally supplement each

FIGURE 7.3
How to Prepare Students for the Criteria of the Rubric

Consider the following questions to help your students practice how to use each of the six criteria.

1. **Issues and Questions**
   a. Given this scenario, what is the most fundamental question at issue?
   b. How can you express the question in several ways to clarify its meaning and scope?
   c. Can you break the question into sub-questions?
   d. Can you identify the type of question you are dealing with (historical, economic, biological, etc.)?
   e. Is there more than one important question to be considered?

2. **Context**
   a. What does the influence of certain types of context (e.g., cultural, social, educational, technological, political, economic, ethical, etc.) on your issue mean to your interpretation and resolution of the issue?
   b. What types of context might influence the issue you are describing?
   c. How do the most relevant contexts influence the issue?
   d. Given the most relevant contexts you have identified for this issue, what are the key concepts to be applied?

3. **Perspectives**
   a. From what point of view are you looking at the issue?
   b. Are you so locked into your point of view that you are unable to see the issue from other points of view?
   c. Must you consider multiple points of view to reason well through the issue at hand?
   d. What are the strengths and weaknesses of your point of view (as well as other's points of view)?
   e. (In case you are writing a critique:) What is the point of view of the author?
   f. What is the frame of reference in this discipline?
   g. Are different worldviews implicit in these different perspectives?

4. **Assumptions**
   a. What are your assumptions, the things you take for granted in a particular claim you make?
   b. What values are your assumptions based on?
   c. Are your assumptions justifiable?
   d. How are your assumptions shaping your point of view?

5. Evidence
   a. What types of evidence are available:
       i.   Empirical data?
       ii. Expert testimonials?
       iii. Anecdotal/personal experiences?
       iv. Theoretical arguments?
   b. What evidence supports your claims?
   c. What evidence opposes your position?
   d. Have you considered all significant evidence relevant to the issue?

6. Implications and Conclusions
   a. Given the main question/issue, what implications does your evidence have for a resolution of the issue?
   b. Are the inferences you draw from your various pieces of evidence consistent with each other?
   c. Is your evidence strong enough to clearly support just one conclusion?
   d. What are the possible positive and negative consequences of your suggested resolution?

---

other. When faculty talk about their courses, they usually talk about course content. Rubrics give them an opportunity to talk about learning outcomes and how to help students achieve these outcomes.

As faculty plan or assess their academic program, rubrics that measure skill and ability development help them track these skills across different courses in the program and even across different disciplines. Rubrics, therefore, help answer the "value-added" question; are students at higher levels of their program performing better on these skills than students at lower levels? If not, does this suggest a lack of systematic teaching along the way, and where in the curriculum would it be best to integrate more practice in these skills?

In the interest of further diagnostics, rubrics also help identify strengths and weaknesses over time, for instance across various cohorts of students moving through a program. A low score on the "assumptions" criterion of the critical-thinking rubric might only be of moderate concern if it happens with one student cohort. If it happens repeatedly with different cohorts of students moving through the program year after year, it almost invariably indicates a systematic weakness in the program that needs to be addressed. The rubric, therefore, not only gives a holistic index of students' critical-thinking skills over time, it also allows sub-domains in that overall skill to be tracked so that corrective actions can be taken, possibly involving multiple courses and faculty.

LEARNING EXPERIENCES IN
BUILDING BLOCKS

TASK 4

Competencies
for TASK 4

TASK 3

Competencies
for TASK 3

*Competencies
Practiced
for TASK 4*

TASK 2

Competencies
for TASK 2

*Competencies
Practiced
for TASK 3*

TASK 1

Competencies
for TASK 1

*Competencies
Practiced
for TASK 2*

PERFORMANCE
CRITERIA FOR
COMP'S - SET 1

PERFORMANCE
CRITERIA FOR
COMP'S - SET 2

PERFORMANCE
CRITERIA FOR
COMP'S - SET 3

PERFORMANCE
CRITERIA FOR
COMP'S - SET 4

8

CONTENT, PART 2: LEARNING EXPERIENCES

OVERVIEW

EXAMPLES OF POOR ASSIGNMENTS

- What is the rationale for traditional assignments?
- Examples of typical assignments that are problematic

AUTHENTIC PERFORMANCE TASKS

- How to think differently about the nature of assignments
- What makes for an authentic performance task?

ASSIGNMENT-CENTERED INSTRUCTION

- The rationale behind "assignment-centered" instruction
- The characteristics of assignment-centeredness

ASSIGNMENT-RELATED COMPETENCIES

- How to determine the competencies necessary for doing an assignment
- An example of competencies needed for certain performance tasks

BUILDING BLOCK DESIGNS

- What are building block designs?
- Four examples of building block formats

Principles for designing effective learning experiences

Student involvement in the pedagogy

- Authentic performance tasks allow for student choice
- Rubrics allow for student–faculty collaboration and for student self-assessment
- Identifying needed competencies helps with self-regulation of student improvement
- Explicit syllabi help students understand the rationale behind a course

Examples of Poor Assignments

What Is the Rationale for Traditional Assignments?

Assignments such as term papers are often given for one main reason, to provide another, more qualitative means to assign student grades besides "objective" class exams and quizzes. In this context, term papers or class projects are seen as tools for diversifying the assessment of student learning, guided by the recognition that some students do better on papers than tests. Assigning papers then becomes a matter of balancing the strengths and weaknesses in students' learning styles. Although this is a reasonable concern, it sells short the true potential of making students work on tasks outside of class. Too often, the chosen tasks appear quite random and only marginally related to the purpose of the course. What follows are some assignment formats that illustrate this point.

Examples of Typical Assignments That Are Problematic

- The Battleship Term Paper

    A colleague at a writing center used this expression to refer to the traditional end-of-semester 20-plus-page paper that would typically cost students an "all-nighter" or two to finish. It is rarely a meaningful, well-integrated task, but requires a painful burst of effort, over which most students procrastinate until they can no longer put it off. At that point, the key purpose of the assignment is to demonstrate to the instructor that the student has acquired, in this or previous classes, the skill of elaborating on a topic in more space than is available on an exam.

- Dead Assignments

    Virtually all the assignments described in this short listing can be called "dead" assignments. Like the Battleship Term Paper, they have one fleeting purpose, to generate a product that can be assigned a significant portion of the course grade, but that has little function for the learning targeted by the course outcomes.

- Misguided Creativity

    Some instructors have identified another purpose of assignments, making the class "fun." They might get students to engage in interesting and creative activities, for example, asking students to produce skits, collect photos or advertisements, create collages in small groups, and so on, and students might enjoy performing these tasks. There is only one drawback; the tasks themselves have little to do with any of the intended learning outcomes. The link is only superficial and does not justify the amount of time spent on the assignment in or out of class.

- Do Somethings

    Occasionally instructors seem content with students showing competence at something . . . anything. They do not provide written instructions for an assignment and only make verbal announcements that are wide open to interpretation. It appears that the instructor's sense of what the assignment should accomplish "jells" as he or she sees what the students have actually produced. At that point, it's too late to formalize it, and the instructor accepts the students' rendition of what they thought the instructor intended. (As variations, the instructor might change the assignment over the course of several class sessions as a result of "negotiating" student objections, or provide a host of "options" for students to choose from.)

- Generics

    Unlike the drugs, these Generics are missing an important ingredient. Student populations at most universities have become more diverse, presenting the opportunity to create rich, contextualized assignments that make use of the students' various experiential backgrounds. Unfortunately, many assignments still ignore these changes and create tasks that are purged of any resemblance to the realities of everyday student lives.

- Cookbook Recipes

    Students like security and often want to be told exactly what to do. Instructors might give in to this understandable request and provide students with model assignments that require little imagination or creativity. The task then becomes little more than a fill-in-the-blank. Model assignments and detailed instructions are useful, but not if they prescribe the ideal that one merely follows to the letter.

- Mind Readers

    Some instructions for assignments read like manifestos in which the instructor lays out his or her philosophy of scholarship and life in general. There are references to academic excellence, intellectual integrity, maybe even quotes from cultural icons that are meant to warn or inspire. But students have to search long and hard through all the verbiage to discover what they are expected to do. The instructions are so implicit that the assignment becomes a guessing game.

Students have to try to get inside the instructor's head to figure out what he or she thinks is worth doing.

- Last-Minute Decisions

     Some instructors underscore the irrelevance of assignments for the course by not including them in the syllabus and announcing that they will be given later, maybe the week before the assignment is due. These instructors might have run out of time designing their course before classes start, or they might first want to get to know the students better before committing to a particular assignment that matches the students' needs. Although the latter sounds like an honorable reason for withholding an assignment, it unfortunately also tends to prevent the assignment from having a significant impact on the course.

Authentic Performance Tasks

How to Think Differently About the Nature of Assignments

There is a different approach to conceiving course assignments. Rather than seeing them as means for diversifying grading, make them an entry point into the field for your students. Students ought to learn what types of problems and issues an academic discipline addresses and how it applies its theoretical knowledge to realistic scenarios. According to Wiggins and McTighe (2005, p. 154), assignments should measure students' true understanding of key course concepts, theories, and procedures. True understanding is hard to assess with multiple-choice test questions. Even essay questions often look more for an intelligent summary of course content than for application of that knowledge to the real world. Therefore, according to Wiggins and McTighe, the best way to measure understanding is by requiring learners to perform "authentic" tasks. Chapter 6 listed Wiggins' six criteria that make a task authentic.

What Makes for an Authentic Performance Task?

The task must:

1. Be realistically contextualized.
2. Require judgment and innovation.
3. Ask the student to "do" the subject.
4. Replicate key challenging situations in which professionals are truly "tested" in their field.

5. Assess the student's ability to use a repertoire of knowledge and skill.
6. Allow appropriate opportunities to rehearse, practice, and get feedback.

A further explanation is in order here; authentic performance tasks are not an exotic sideline of recent educational theory. Starting with John Dewey's classic 1938 volume, *Experience and Education,* a growing line of theory and research has supported the importance of incorporating authentic tasks in education. These tasks are not merely relevant for assessing the depth and adequacy of student learning. Authentic performance is also recommended for increasing complex skills by honing them in the context of real-life activities, improving students' intrinsic motivation to learn, and supporting students' social and intellectual growth and development.

Related theoretical approaches include Situated Cognition, Cognitive Apprenticeship, Reflection-in-Action, Transformative Learning, Anchored Instruction, Self-Directed Learning, Experiential Learning, as well as Project/Problem-Based Learning. Especially the rise of adult learning theory has added a focus on developmental objectives to the learning process rather than being contented with the mechanisms of cognitive skill gains. Kathleen Taylor, Catherine Marienau, and Morris Fiddler (2000) surveyed adult educators on three continents to find out what types of developmental goals they held for their adult learners. From those responses, the authors generated five dimensions of what they call "developmental intentions" that underlie the teaching of adult learners in particular. Development is marked by the learner's movement toward:

1. Knowing as a dialogical process (e.g., associating truth not with static fact but with contexts and relationships).
2. Dialogical relationship to oneself (e.g., questioning critically the validity or worth of one's pursuit).
3. Being a continuous learner (e.g., setting one's own learning goals, being goal-directed, and being habitual in learning).
4. Self-agency and self-authorship (e.g., taking action toward one's potential while acknowledging one's limitations).
5. Connection with others (e.g., contributing one's voice to a collective endeavor).

One of the more frequently used approaches to putting these priorities into practice is Project-Based Learning. Similar to authentic performance tasks, "projects" are defined as "realistic, not school-like," "student-driven to some significant degree," "involving students in a constructive investigation," and "focused on questions or problems that 'drive' students to encounter (and struggle with) the central concepts and principles of the discipline" (Thomas, 2000, pp. 3–4). Although the research on these approaches is still fairly young, especially in the college environment, a number of positive results have been found. Probably the most comprehensive review of such early research was conducted by John W. Thomas (2000), with much smaller reviews coming from CELL (2009), Intel Teach Program (2007), and Edutopia (2001). Results from these reviews of the research suggest that students benefit from project-based learning with:

- Growth in self-reliance and improved attitudes toward learning.
- Academic gains equal or better than those generated by other teaching models.
- Development of complex skills, such as critical thinking, problem-solving, collaborating.
- A broader range of learning opportunities, providing a strategy for engaging culturally diverse learners. (Intel Teach Program, 2007)

Assignment-Centered Instruction

The Rationale Behind "Assignment-Centered" Instruction

A logical extension of the practice of assigning authentic performance tasks leads to a revision in how to look at course design as a whole. If true understanding is best measured by creating authentic tasks that students perform, then it makes sense to move away from course design as the process of simply outlining course content in some logical progression. Instead, courses should center on a series of assignments by which students learn to apply the content they are acquiring along the way.

Barbara Walvoord and Virginia Anderson (1998) have been advocates for "assignment-centered course design" in higher education in recent years. In their view, the course-planning process begins by focusing on the assignments, tests, and exams that will both teach and test what the teacher most wants students to know. Research suggests that the assignment-centered course enhances students' higher-order reasoning and critical thinking more effectively than do courses built around text, lecture, and content coverage (Kurfiss, 1988).

The Characteristics of Assignment-Centeredness

The assignment-centered course creates a skeleton built of the main assignments across the semester. Especially the first assignments are designed as *building blocks* that help students gradually develop complex skills. Key characteristics of the assignment-centered course include:

1. *Do not ask, "What should I cover in this course?" but "What should my students learn to do?"*

     This is the main tenet of outcomes-based learning, in which passive content knowledge that has not been turned into tasks students can perform is not considered a productive outcome.

2. *Select assignments/activities (e.g., papers, tests, projects) that teach and test this learning.*

     Class assignments and activities need to be aligned with the intended learning outcomes of the course. Assignments then become not just a means of assigning grades but of teaching knowledge and skills.

3. *Spread the assignments throughout your course.*

     The "Battleship Term Paper" discussed earlier represents the antithesis to this approach. A single, long assignment is left usually until the end of the semester with little or no function for student learning throughout the course.

4. *Structure your course in such a way that early assignments function as skills building blocks for later ones.*

     For example, instead of requesting a full lab report, have students write only the introduction as a first assignment, then add more parts for each subsequent lab report.

5. *Provide clear and detailed instruction sheets for all assignments.*

     The "Do-Something's" and the "Mind Reader" assignments described in the opening of this chapter illustrate how this guideline is often violated. Students moving from class to class, instructor to instructor, and (in General Education courses) from discipline to discipline, will have difficulties interpreting one-sentence instructions that might not even be given in writing. (Walvoord & Anderson, 1998, pp. 26–38)

Assignment-Related Competencies

How to Determine the Competencies Necessary for Doing an Assignment

Part of an idea-based learning approach is that instructors must be cognizant of the key competencies that go into performing a complex task. As we arrive at that point in the course design process where assignments must be aligned with the course learning outcomes, we can finally demonstrate how the different pieces of the Backward Course Design fit together, starting with the big ideas, enduring understandings, and learning outcomes, moving to assignments and the rubrics that make these assignments assessable, and finally ending up with the competencies that need to be developed in carefully designed learning experiences, so that students can perform well on these assignments. The sequence includes the following steps:

1. Select the most relevant big ideas of the discipline (chapter 3).
2. Derive appropriate enduring understandings from these big ideas.
3. Craft a manageable number of learning outcomes from these enduring understandings.
4. Determine which authentic performance tasks can best assess the extent to which the students are achieving the learning outcomes (chapter 6). NOTE: Steps 3 and 4 require careful "negotiating," where one informs the other and vice versa in a process of reaching an optimum match between the two.
5. Given the student population for this course, identify the most common barriers (developmental, attitudinal, cultural, and cognitive) that might get in the way of the students' conceptual understanding of the course content (chapter 4).
6. In view of these common barriers, identify the essential questions and the guiding concepts that have to be addressed under each learning outcome (chapter 5).
7. Create rubrics for these tasks with specific criteria that show students what is important when performing the tasks (chapter 7).
8. Select a manageable number of competencies that are particularly important for your students to work on in order to live up to these performance criteria (chapter 8).
9. Create learning experiences around these abilities so that students get sufficient practice developing them.
10. Sequence these learning experiences in meaningful building blocks throughout the semester.

An Example of Competencies Needed for Certain Performance Tasks

Figure 8.1 illustrates Steps 6 through 9, with the psychology course on Motivational Theories that has been showcased in the previous chapters. This course has one main performance task with five parts: Identify issue and target population for a research project, create research design, collect data, analyze data, and present findings. For each of these components or assignments, a set of performance criteria was created that are listed in the middle column. The column on the right lists a select set of competencies that are prerequisites for mastering the performance task.

The listed competencies are merely a short selection of what is needed to competently perform the task. However, they are the instructor's best estimate of where the students in this class need the most practice and what can be accomplished in the limited time the course provides. The three competencies underlying the first part of the performance task shall illustrate this.

The performance task of doing a qualitative evaluation study about the motivational mind-sets of the inhabitants of a retirement home is linked with all the learning outcomes of the course. As they observe how the retirees handle the challenges at this stage of their lives, students become aware of motivational mechanisms in the people they observe as well as in themselves. They have the opportunity to observe others, reflect upon themselves, critique the theoretical concepts of the course, and learn about a variety of methodological issues involved in conducting this type of observational research.

The first part of the authentic performance task, identifying a researchable issue within a segment of the target population, includes at least three competencies with which students tend to have difficulties: Coming up with a personal interest that makes this target population relevant to them, brainstorming access issues to the field, and previewing relevant theoretical concepts that guide the development of important questions to ask during the research. Competency "a" requires students to address the notion of selecting research targets for a purpose whose relevance they can defend in public discourse. Competency "b" enables them to determine the aspects that might make access to the target population difficult as well as strategies that will help overcome these difficulties. And competency "c" allows them to make an educated guess about relevant theoretical aspects before they actually have all the information needed about the research context.

This example illustrates how the steps in the backward course design are completed. The *big ideas* and *enduring understandings* allow for the creation of meaningful *learning outcomes*, as long as those are matched up with engaging *performance tasks*. The performance tasks are guided by *rubrics*, which provide the criteria for what *competencies* students need to develop. Those

FIGURE 8.1
PY-64: Performance Tasks, Criteria, and Key Competencies

Performance Task	Task Performance Criteria	Key Competencies
PART 1: **Identify issue and target population** for a psychology consulting project. The target population (e.g., residents at a retirement home, high school seniors, a struggling sports team, volunteers in a charitable organization) experiences motivational issues.	1. Explains reason for choosing main issue and target population 2. Considers problems with access to the field 3. Identifies related motivation-theoretical concepts and essential questions	a. Identifying personal interest (in the target population) b. Brainstorming different types of issues with access to the target population, such as legal, logistical, personality-related, etc. c. Previewing relevant concepts and essential questions (by skimming textbook/syllabus)
PART 2: **Create an effective research design.** It is to include an observational phase related to the context in which the target population functions, and also interviews with select respondents.	1. Explains how to get access to respondents 2. Establishes workable observation and interview schedule 3. Reviews relevant literature to provide focus for observation and interviews 4. Creates interview guide	a. Creating a written introduction of self and of project for target institution's administration b. Brainstorming relevant questions c. Estimating appropriate times needed for observations and interviews d. Designing strategies for identifying and approaching respondents e. Writing and sequencing interview questions f. Identifying key variables involved in the context g. Identifying context-related research literature and summarizing key points

FIGURE 8.1 (Continued)

PART 3: **Collect data** to be recorded in a field journal.	1. Implements observation and interview schedule 2. Takes proper field notes 3. Separates field notes from subjective reflections	a. Preparing for appropriate inquiry and data documentation methods b. Using least-obtrusive techniques for observing, taking notes, and recording c. Properly organizing data for later review d. Keeping interviews/observations on schedule
PART 4: **Analyze data**, based on the literature presented in this course. Reflect on systematic shortcomings of your research.	1. Categorizes data into appropriate clusters 2. Connects observations with appropriate theoretical concepts 3. Identifies social and personal implications 4. Reflects on potential shortcomings of the research	a. Establishing a coding schema b. Linking concepts to real-world applications c. Connecting concepts with each other d. Questioning assumptions e. Identifying different points of view f. Generalizing without overreaching
PART 5: **Present findings** in a class presentation (to client and class). Recommendations to address observed issues are requested by client.	1. Briefly outlines the study's procedures and problems 2. Summarizes key findings, as they relate to motivation theory 3. Explains recommendations for the client	a. Judging applicability of theoretical concepts to practical research contexts b. Identifying missing or inaccessible information c. Brainstorming alternative explanations for every conclusion generated

competencies determine the practice opportunities that make up the bulk of the course's *learning experiences.*

There is one more step to take. That step involves the sequencing of these learning activities.

Building Block Designs

What Are Building Block Designs?

Assignment-centered instruction does not just distinguish itself by designing the course as a skeleton of different assignments throughout the semester. To be more effective, especially for students at lower levels, these assignments should also be organized in such a way that they contribute cumulatively to a growing sophistication in the student. They thereby represent a developmental design, in which each individual assignment functions as a building block for the overall learning goal. The following pages describe four different formats, with brief illustrations as to how they might be used.

Four Examples of Building Block Formats

Stepwise Design

This format (see figure 8.2) is the prototype of a building block design. A large assignment, such as a research paper, is broken down into several pieces that are assigned one at a time. For example, students might initially be asked to define a topic for their research. They brainstorm, do some preliminary reading to help generate a focus for the project, and then write up what they have done and the rationale it provides for the pieces to follow. The purpose of such a procedure is to organize what might otherwise seem like an overwhelming task into manageable subtasks. After each of these subtasks, there are opportunities for instructor feedback that allow the student to take corrective action. Each additional assignment then builds upon the previous one and on the insights gained from it. This allows the student to grow over time and eventually master the whole complex task, gaining increasing confidence and understanding during the semester.

Such a design can be adapted to virtually any discipline. It does not have to involve a large assignment that is broken into smaller pieces. It could also be done with a set of separate assignments, in which each one, though standing on its own, gives the students an opportunity to practice skills, on which the following assignment can then expand.

FIGURE 8.2
Stepwise Design

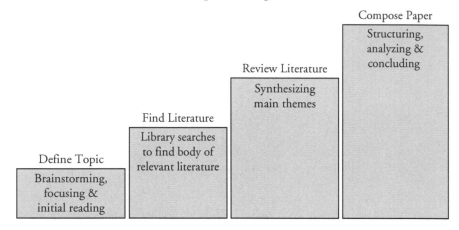

Design characteristics:
- Builds increased sophistication in the student.
- Breaks a large assignment into smaller, more manageable parts.

Especially usable for:
- Larger research/term papers.
- Complex skills for the humanities and social sciences, but also projects in other disciplines.

Process and Inquiry Design

This is also a stepwise design in that the different pieces contribute to the eventual accomplishment of a larger, complex task (see figure 8.3). The difference in this format is that the types of skills practiced in the various steps are qualitatively different from each other. The skills practiced during the initial assignment(s) are "process skills," such as learning to work effectively in a team, mastering basic lab procedures, acquiring fundamental skills in conducting field interviews, and so on. They provide the necessary foundations for subsequent assignments that focus on inquiry skills (e.g., for a research project, lab experiment, or field study) that could not be obtained had it not been for the prior acquisition of the process skills.

FIGURE 8.3
Process and Inquiry Design

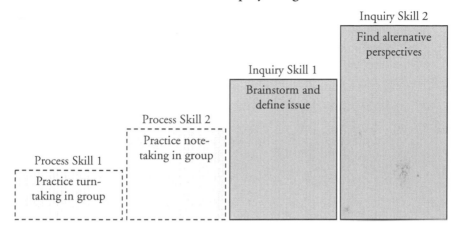

Design characteristics:
- The initial assignment(s) provide students with process skills (such as working productively in small groups) that are necessary for the inquiry skills required later on in the actual assignment.
- The process resembles that of the Stepwise Design in that each element is the stepping stone for the next one.

Especially usable for:
- Creating a preparatory phase in which to teach students the basic skills needed for later complex assignments.
- Can be used for almost any discipline, in particular in the introductory phases of a program.

Cluster Design

Although the different assignments in the cluster design also contribute to a growing sophistication in the student, they are not as clearly sequential and stepwise as the previous two designs (see figure 8.4). An example of the cluster design would be reading logs or reflective journals. Each time the student engages in this task, the purpose and procedures are virtually identical. However, each written entry demands a response for a different stimulus and, over time, students are challenged to become more proficient at focusing on what is most meaningful to them, thereby gradually developing their own voice. Of course, for these to qualify as "building blocks," the instructor needs to plan for a cumulative effect, that is, for opportunities to periodically review, synthesize, and learn from the writing activities as they occur.

Design characteristics:
- Each assignment contributes equally to building a larger, complex skill. The building blocks have no inherent hierarchical structure.
- Provides a variety of practice opportunities for different facets of the skill.

Especially usable for:
- Teaching related writing skills.
- Teaching a similar type of skills in the research lab, such as various forms of double-blind experiments.

FIGURE 8.4
Cluster Design

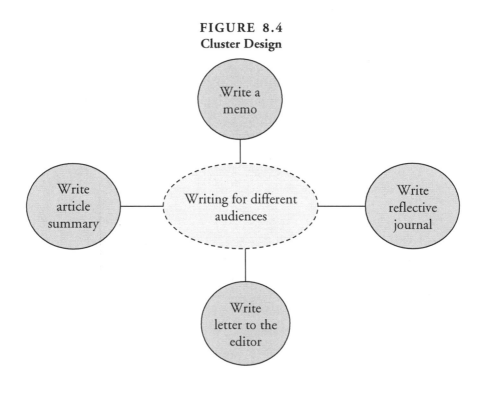

Inquiry/Experiential Learning Design

As illustrated in figure 8.5, this approach connects several real-life (or simulated) activities with one or more levels of reflection and synthesis about these activities. Students start by doing a practical investigation in a realistic context, for example, interviewing a respondent or observing a particular situation or event. Their activity then becomes the object of a summarizing task that allows a first reflection on the information they have gathered in the field. This two-step process is repeated one or more times. The results provide the basis for a final synthesizing activity, such as a paper or a class presentation. A good example for this procedure comes from cultural anthropology. The student anthropologist goes into the field repeatedly to collect data, writes them up each time on returning from the field, and eventually synthesizes his or her findings in a report to be shared with colleagues. This procedure is similar to the stepwise design. The difference is that each initial step consists of multiple repetitions that create the complexity of information needed for the final step.

FIGURE 8.5
Inquiry/Experiential Learning Design

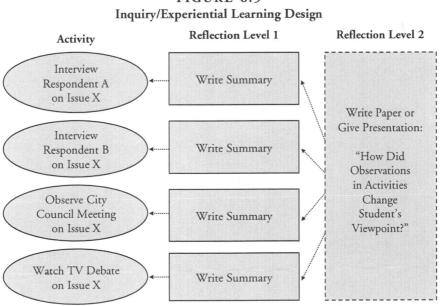

Design characteristics:
- Each assignment contributes a unique experience.
- All (sub)assignments will eventually be synthesized into a larger task.

Especially usable for:
- Teaching with experiential learning.
- Getting students involved in field-based research.
- Almost any discipline.

Principles for Designing Effective Learning Experiences

Effective learning experiences produce more than factual content knowledge. They translate intended learning outcomes into activities that challenge students to develop an in-depth understanding of how content can be applied in meaningful contexts. The most important learning experiences are therefore arranged around authentic performance tasks that require students to perform (or at least to simulate) what true professionals in the field are expected to do on a routine basis. This is a tall order, but it helps students make sense of the concepts, procedures, and attitudes they are learning.

As a consequence, effective instruction is less a result of what the teacher says and more of what the students practice. Successful learning is based on doing, not on listening, although some listening can be part of the tasks. Effective instruction is, therefore, assignment-centered, where students practice their skills and transform their knowledge into contextualized understanding. The function of the teacher is to create appropriate learning tasks and environments (Barr & Tagg, 1995). Good instructors are sophisticated observers of their students' learning hurdles. They analyze which competencies students have and which ones they lack and then design practice activities to move them to the next level. Creating assignments in building blocks makes it possible to systematically help students grow throughout a course. The following principles summarize the important elements for creating effective learning experiences.

1. Make teaching assignment-centered so that students need to do the task rather than just talk about it.
2. Break complex performance tasks into smaller building blocks that are spread strategically across the semester so that each task prepares students for the next one.

3. Cycle through the same challenging ideas multiple times and in different course contexts to improve the chances for new ideas to be anchored in existing knowledge, enabling understanding to emerge gradually.
4. Provide periodic opportunities for reflection and self-assessment so that students recognize their progress but also identify where they are still falling short.
5. Challenge students to process complex and difficult ideas in groups that support frequent role change between explaining their own and listening to others' understanding of those ideas.
6. Require students to work through new ideas by having them defend positions that contradict their current beliefs, so that they learn to better understand other people's perspectives.
7. Constantly assess the difficulties students have in their conceptual understanding of the content so that you can create appropriate practice opportunities to overcome those difficulties.
8. Provide a safe environment that encourages intellectual risk taking and in which learning from mistakes is supported.

Student Involvement in the Pedagogy

Authentic Performance Tasks Allow for Student Choice

The more students understand this instructional approach, the better they are likely to perform. The best way for students to gain that understanding is to provide choices and involve them in the decision making. Wherever possible, students should be given choices in the authentic performance tasks they do. As the example in figure 8.1 illustrates, students in the Theories of Motivation course have a choice of target populations that they wish to observe. Students may choose according to access to a given population, but they may also choose according to how interested they are in working with one population versus another.

Rubrics Allow for Student–Faculty Collaboration and for Student Self-Assessment

The previous chapter suggested direct student involvement in designing the rubrics that assess the quality of their work. There is no better way for students to understand which criteria determine performance than to participate in the definition of those criteria. It opens students' eyes to the different dimensions of a task, and it also helps instructors understand the intellectual maturity level of their students. Both are equally important.

Identifying Needed Competencies Helps With Self-Regulation of Student Improvement

The same is true for having students explore the competencies needed to master the intellectual challenges of performing a complex performance task. One of the key incentives for helping students improve their performance is to help them recognize the progress they make over time. This can be done over the timeframe of a course, but it is even more beneficial if it extends beyond the limits of a single course and applies to their whole program. Chapter 10 describes the capabilities that electronic learning portfolios offer for enabling students to document and reflect on their entire college career. This supports insights far beyond what single courses have to offer.

Explicit Syllabi Help Students Understand the Rationale Behind a Course

Finally, the detailed course design efforts described in the previous chapters offer the opportunity of significantly improving the quality of course syllabi. Instead of focusing on rules, threats, and penalties for student "misbehavior," the syllabus can actually be used to explain the kind of learning that a course sets out to accomplish. The final part of chapter 9, together with the sample syllabus in the appendix, illustrates how a substantive course outline can be used to engage students in discussions of what should be accomplished and the means for doing so.

COURSE DESIGN COMPONENTS AND STEPS

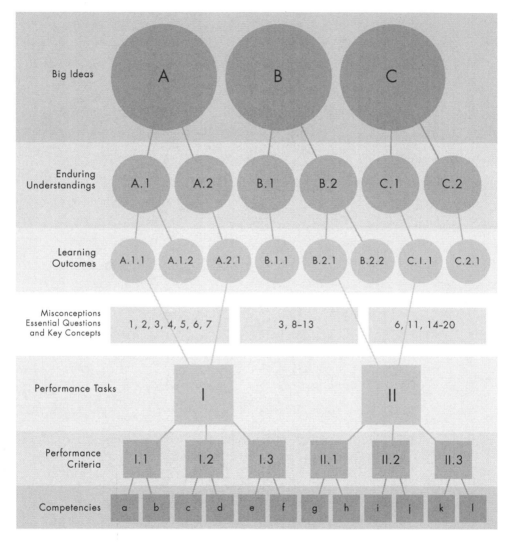

9

COURSE DESIGN DOCUMENT

OVERVIEW

WHY CREATE COURSE DESIGN DOCUMENTS?

- The problem of multiple sections taught by different instructors
- Syllabi provide no conceptual framework for a course

ELEMENTS OF THE COURSE DESIGN DOCUMENT

- Step 1: Big ideas
- Step 2: Enduring understandings
- Step 3: Learning outcomes
- Step 4: Authentic performance tasks
- Step 5: Common barriers and misconceptions
- Step 6: Essential questions
- Step 7: Guiding concepts
- Step 8: Task performance criteria
- Step 9: Key competencies

SAMPLE COURSE DESIGN DOCUMENT: PSYCHOLOGY 624—THEORIES OF MOTIVATION

SUMMARY OF COURSE DESIGN FEATURES AND BENEFITS

TRANSLATING THE COURSE DESIGN DOCUMENT INTO A SYLLABUS

Why Create Course Design Documents?

The Problem of Multiple Sections Taught by Different Instructors

I ended chapter 2 by arguing that college classes need more than the syllabus as the main document that describes what happens in a given course. We suffer from a serious lack of systematic blueprints that communicate, not just to our students but among instructors and whole departments, how learning is organized in each class, what is to be accomplished in the various units that make up the curriculum, and how we know what has been achieved by the end of the course. All too often, a review of the syllabi of different sections of the same course reveals a lack of agreement among the various instructors teaching it on what the learning outcomes for a course should be. Faculty might have a vague understanding of what needs to be "covered" in an Introduction to American National Government course or in a course on Contemporary Issues in Mass Media, but there is very little explicit deliberation among them about what exactly the students should take away from these courses.

Syllabi Provide No Conceptual Framework for a Course

Part of the problem is that the one document that faculty create for their course, the syllabus, addresses little else but a brief content overview in the form of a topics outline, a listing of the assignments and tests that can be expected ("details to be provided at a later point in the semester"), policies describing what student behavior the instructor does or does not tolerate in the classroom, and the relative weights for the graded course activities. Unfortunately little of this information addresses the questions that should be asked about the conceptual framework of a course, so that one can determine exactly how it fits into the overall curriculum.

Even if all instructors of the various course sections were to teach from the same syllabus—a relatively uncommon procedure in many departments—that syllabus would provide precious little guidance for how students in these sections might reach the same learning outcomes. Things get even more difficult when it comes to reaching coherence across the courses of a whole program, not to mention a curriculum as large as General Education that crosses disciplinary boundaries. Relatively random lists of course topics do not indicate what students should be able to do with the knowledge they acquire in their field. Even course learning outcomes are difficult to map onto the broad goals that a department establishes for itself. Besides, it is often impossible to identify how the course outcomes are actually transformed into the specific learning experiences and assessment procedures that constitute the semester's work.

Syllabi do not define these types of structures and connections. At best, they outline an implied logic that the instructor has put on delivering the content. This is what Wiggins and McTighe (2005) have called "the logic of the content" that does not in itself reveal "the logic of learning (or performing with) content." Whereas the logic of the content can be fairly linear and hierarchical, the logic of learning the content has to consider the students and their need to go back and forth between the details and the big picture. Students make connections over time. They need opportunities to practice and make mistakes. In order to build a deep understanding, they need to "do" a subject rather than just "learn about" it. A course document that reflects this logic of *learning* content needs to provide the big picture, including how other parts of the course relate to it. It needs to recognize the kinds of problems students are likely to encounter with the content, and it needs to give an idea of the tasks students will engage in as they "do" the subject and perform with the content to integrate it into their conceptual schema.

The model presented in the previous chapters outlines ways of interconnecting the main components of a course and achieving alignment as the course design moves from the general to the specific:

- A systematic derivation of learning outcomes starts with a small number of *big ideas* that characterize a discipline. Each big idea is subdivided into *enduring understandings* that contribute the broad themes for the course. Each theme provides the basis for one or more *learning outcomes* that are thereby clearly grounded in the conceptual foundations of the discipline.
- Learning outcomes are also shaped by the *authentic performance tasks* assigned to students, because those tasks set limits on how the learning outcomes can be implemented in a given course. Therefore, both the learning outcomes and the performance tasks need to be designed together.
- Once this foundation is laid, more detailed decisions can be made. Common student *misconceptions* regarding course content are determined next. They then allow for the formulation of *essential questions* and *guiding concepts*.
- *Learning activities* are organized around one or more complex *performance tasks*, requiring students to demonstrate their understanding

of the material and thereby achievement of the intended learning outcomes.

- The final step closes the loop between outcomes and assessment. It breaks down the performance tasks into distinct *performance criteria* as well as *key competencies* that enable students to be successful at the performance tasks and allow faculty to measure the learning specified in the course outcomes.

This model of course design achieves curricular alignment by systematically breaking down key course components into their constituent elements. The result is a course that can demonstrate in detail how the different parts relate to each other and create the intended results for student learning.

In addition to the crucial task of demonstrating curricular alignment, the course design document should also be practical and not unduly complicated, and it should be sensitive to the academic authority faculty require to be effective teachers. To summarize, we need a course design document that:

- Explains the conceptual framework for a course.
- Is sufficient as a tool to communicate the essence of a course to instructors across sections, the curriculum, and even disciplines.
- Is concise enough to allow a relatively quick overview.
- Determines the crucial common elements while leaving enough flexibility for individual instructors to teach to their strengths and personal styles.

The previous chapters elaborated on the different components that are part of such a document. The nine-step process outlined in this chapter is a short summary of the key ideas presented in previous chapters. They are intended both as a recap of these ideas and a stand-alone document that faculty can use to design their course documents.

Elements of the Course Design Document

The following stepwise procedure suggests how to build a course design document that fulfills the requirements previously summarized. Figures 9.1 and 9.2 provide an illustration of such a course design document, using the psychology course that has served as an example throughout this book. Steps 1–3 and 5–7 are framed by one of the learning outcomes, to which all the other steps are logically tied. Therefore, the rows in figure 9.1 are all defined at the level of the learning outcomes (this is graphically illustrated in figure 9.3).

Steps 4, 8, and 9, presented in figure 9.2, use another element as the defining unit, the authentic performance task. The tasks that students have to perform to show their mastery of the learning outcomes typically involve more than one outcome. Because authentic performance tasks are the measure of learning outcomes, it seems appropriate to use them for outlining the final step in the course design process, the determination of which competencies are most important (and frequently underdeveloped) for students to do well on those tasks. We will look at these steps in sequence.

The key for creating a course design document is the process of deriving meaningful learning outcomes that are capable of giving everything that happens in a course purpose and cohesion. Defining good learning outcomes for a course can be difficult. First of all, one has to find the right scope. Course outcomes are located between program goals and daily lesson outcomes; they are not as broad as the former or as narrow as the latter. Second, every field and topic has an almost endless number of possibilities for learning outcomes. And finally, learning outcomes are not confined to knowledge. In fact, knowledge is usually embedded in a good learning outcome that might focus on a skill or an attitude, such as developing a habit for skeptical questioning of assumptions. To define the most relevant learning outcomes for a course, the first four steps in this document will be helpful. They form a funnel process that guides you to become progressively more concrete about which learning outcomes are appropriate for the course.

Step 1: Big Ideas

First, review the list of program goals your course is expected to fit into. Select those goals that are relevant to the proposed course. A good way to arrive at meaningful learning outcomes is by starting with the big ideas in your discipline. (See examples in figure 9.1). Nobody has time to teach everything there is to know in a given field, so we want to focus on the glue that holds a field together, the truly important meta-concepts and theories that make the transfer of learning possible. These big ideas will then function as the "conceptual lenses" that make it easy to move across new knowledge domains without feeling lost.

Big Ideas characterize a discipline. That does not imply that they have to be unique to one discipline. Some big ideas might be shared by several

FIGURE 9.1

Course Design Document Part 1—Psychology 624: Theories of Motivation

Big Ideas	Enduring Understandings	Learning Outcomes	Misconceptions	Essential Questions	Guiding Concepts
Motivators of behavior	Behavior is influenced by *external* incentives and *internal* needs.	1) Students become aware of previously *unnoticed factors* influencing their own and others' intellectual *curiosity*, desire to *achieve*, and their *self-concept*.	1. Rewards are good. 2. Successful people are good at setting goals for themselves. 3. Self-esteem is built through other people's praise.	1. How can rewards undermine motivation? 2. Is goal-setting enough to increase achievement? 3. How can low self-esteem be changed?	1. Extrinsic motivation 2. Intrinsic motivation 3. Perceived locus of control 4. Reward and punishment 5. Optimal challenge 6. Achievement motivation 7. Goal setting 8. Self-efficacy 9. Learned helplessness
	Motivation involves the interaction of *emotion* and *cognition*.	2) Explain how cognitive mechanisms can help people overcome motivational tendencies such as *anger* and *defeatism*.	4. Behavior is either determined by emotion or cognition. 5. Defense mechanisms are bad.	4. Can emotions (e.g., anger) be controlled by cognitions? How does what we think influence what we feel? 5. Do we need to create a false sense of reality to maintain our "sanity"?	1. Perceived locus of control 2. Self-concept 3. Cognitive dissonance 4. Identity 5. Learned helplessness 6. Attribution errors 7. Ego-defenses

Individual differences	Motivation varies in *intensity* and *type*.	3) Recognize people's reasons for *seeking or avoiding* certain behaviors or experiences.	6. Studying (in school) is boring. 7. Stress is bad. 8. Competition is good.	6. Why are many people "bored" with their jobs/school/life? 7. Which experiences are "stressful"? 8. Is risk-taking necessary for feeling alive?	1. Temperament 2. Optimal arousal 3. Homeostasis 4. Sensation seeking 5. Extraversion vs. introversion
	Motivation varies across people from different *cultural backgrounds*.	4) Interpret *individual differences* within cultural contexts.	9. We all have the same psychological needs. 10. Key values are universal (e.g., individualism, achievement, competition, self-actualization). 11. Children need both parents to grow into healthy adults.	9. Why do different people develop different explanations for what happens to them? 10. Why do people in some cultures develop a higher need for achievement than people in other cultures? 11. Does single parenthood lead to maladjustment in children? 12. Are attachment patterns different across cultures?	1. Values 2. Individualism vs. collectivism 3. Competition vs. collaboration 4. Work ethic 5. Culture 6. Optimism vs. pessimism

FIGURE 9.1 (Continued)

Big Ideas	Enduring Understandings	Learning Outcomes	Misconceptions	Essential Questions	Guiding Concepts
Psychological theorizing	Research on motivation has moved from grand to mini-theories.	5) Identify practical implications of *different* motivation-theoretical *approaches*.	12. The science of psychology must have universal "laws." 13. Every behavior has one true cause.	13. Do multiple "mini-theories" explain human behavior better than comprehensive attempts at theory-building? 14. What is the difference between a motivational principle and a motivational theory?	Mini-theories for: 1. Self-concept 2. Belonging and attachment 3. Curiosity 4. Achievement 5. Ego defenses 6. Arousal
	*Self-*reports (on which parts of motivation theories are based) are *susceptible to errors*.	6) Learn to reflect on causes for own behavior while being critical of possible shortcomings of such *introspection*.	14. I have direct access to the causes for my actions. 15. If an explanation matches with our own experiences, it must be true.	15. Can we observe the causes of our actions directly? 16. Where are introspections deceiving? (See attribution theory.) 17. What motivates you, and how is that similar or different from what motivates others?	1. Introspection 2. Attribution and schema 3. Causality 4. Correlation 5. Multiple realities 6. Logical fallacies

Qualitative Research	Qualitative research involves *multiple measures*.	7) Design and conduct a small qualitative *research study*.	16. Interview statements are objective data. 17. Behavioral observations are neutral.	18. How does the question format influence the information value of the response? 19. How can you tell whether interviewees tell the truth? 20. How do observers in the field establish trust with those they observe? 21. How generalizable are data from one context to another?	1. Ethnographic interview 2. Triangulation 3. Participant observation 4. Causality

Note: Observe how the different elements across the columns are interconnected, in particular look at the close relationship between Essential Questions, Misconceptions, Learning Outcomes, and Performance Tasks.

FIGURE 9.2

Course Design Document Part 2—Psychology 624: Theories of Motivation

Learning Outcomes	Performance Task	Task Performance Criteria	Key Competencies
# 2, 3, 4	PART 1: **Identify issue and target population** for a psychology consulting project. The target population (e.g., residents at a retirement home, high school seniors, a struggling sports team, volunteers in a charitable organization) experiences lack of motivation.	1. Explains reason for choosing main issue and target population 2. Considers problems with access to the field 3. Identifies related motivation-theoretical concepts and essential questions	a. Identifying personal interest (in the target population) b. Brainstorming different types of issues with access to the target population, such as legal, logistical, personality-related, and so on c. Previewing relevant concepts and essential questions (by skimming text book/syllabus
#7	PART 2: **Create an effective research design.** It is to include an observational phase related to the context in which the target population functions and interviews with select respondents.	1. Explains how to get access to respondents 2. Establishes workable observation and interview schedule 3. Reviews relevant literature to provide focus for observation and interviews 4. Creates interview guide	a. Creating a written introduction of self and of project for target institution's administration b. Brainstorming relevant questions c. Estimating appropriate times needed for observations and interviews d. Designing strategies for identifying and approaching respondents e. Writing and sequencing interview questions f. Identifying key variables involved in the context g. Identifying context-related research literature and summarizing key points

# 6, 7	PART 3: **Collect data** to be recorded in a field journal.	1. Implements observation and interview schedule 2. Takes proper field notes 3. Separates field notes from subjective reflections	a. Preparing for appropriate inquiry and data documentation methods b. Using least-obtrusive techniques for observing, taking notes, and recording c. Properly organizing data for later review d. Keeping interviews/observations on schedule
# 1–6	PART 4: **Analyze data,** based on the literature presented in this course. Reflect on systematic shortcomings of your research.	1. Categorizes data into appropriate clusters 2. Connects observations with appropriate theoretical concepts 3. Identifies social and personal implications 4. Reflects on potential shortcomings of the research	a. Establishing a coding schema b. Linking concepts to real-world applications c. Connecting concepts with each other d. Questioning assumptions e. Identifying different points of view f. Generalizing without overreaching
# 1–4	PART 5: **Present findings** in a class presentation (to client and class). Recommendations to address observed issues are requested by client.	1. Briefly outlines the study's procedures and problems 2. Summarizes key findings, as they relate to motivation theory 3. Explains recommendations for the client	a. Judging applicability of theoretical concepts to practical research contexts b. Identifying missing or inaccessible information c. Brainstorming alternative explanations for every conclusion generated

FIGURE 9.3
Course Design Document Template

Big Ideas	Enduring Understandings	Learning Outcomes	Common Misconceptions	Essential Questions	Guiding Concepts
A.	A.1.	A.1.a.			
	A.2.	A.2.a.			
B.	B.1.	B.1.a.			
	B.2.	B.2.a.			
C.	C.1.	C.1.a.			
	C.2.	C.2.a.			
		C.2.b.			

disciplines and thus connect fields with each other. For example, the scientific method, as a big idea, is shared across the natural sciences and even with paradigms in certain social sciences. This makes it particularly relevant for General Education courses, because students can compare similarities as well as differences in the ways that disciplines use this big idea, which ultimately allows for more transfer of learning.

When selecting big ideas for a course, the obvious questions to ask are: Is this idea relevant for this particular course level? Is this idea equally relevant for majors and nonmajors, or is it only relevant for majors? Certain big ideas might be crucial for someone starting off in a discipline, but of marginal interest for students who will never move beyond this one course.

How many big ideas should a course address? The answer depends on the complexity of the ideas, but generally speaking, the reason for starting course design with big ideas is to begin to limit the universe of what to cover. Two or three big ideas can be perfectly sufficient for a course. In Step 2, each big idea will be examined for typically more than one enduring understanding, and in Step 3 those understandings can further be divided into different learning outcomes. Three big ideas could therefore easily generate six, nine, or more learning outcomes, which quickly exceeds what a course can reasonably address in one semester.

Step 2: Enduring Understandings

Whereas the big ideas within the disciplines are often encapsulated in one or two word terms (e.g., *Equity*, *Nature vs. Nurture*, *Scientific Method*, *Natural Selection*), enduring understandings are more specific derivations from these ideas, key elements of their definitions, applications, or implications (see examples in figure 9.1). Enduring understandings are generalizations that are central to a discipline and transferable to new situations; they have lasting value beyond the classroom. They are what students should understand and be able to use years after the class is over and most of the details have been forgotten. Although they might have characteristics that are discipline-specific, they also often have strong similarities with other disciplines, which allows for interdisciplinary comparison and collaboration.

Step 3: Learning Outcomes

Once enduring understandings have been derived from the big ideas, it is time to define a limited number of learning outcomes that address the key aspects of the enduring understandings. Besides being limited in scope, learning outcomes need to incorporate the following characteristics:

- *Student-focused:* Outcomes should be phrased from the perspective of what students will be able *to do*, e.g., "By the end of this course, students will be able to design/analyze/compose/compare and contrast/and so on."
- *Emphasis on higher-order thinking skills:* Don't just expect students to "understand" or "remember" content. Challenge them to learn how to do something with the knowledge they are to acquire.
- *Measurable:* Make sure that achievement of the learning outcomes can be measured in some form, whether it is in the form of a test, a paper, a presentation, a performance, and so on. Outcomes should be phrased with a view toward a product that students need to provide as evidence of their learning.
- *Concrete:* Sometimes syllabi seem to express merely some general hopes that instructors have for what students should get out of a course (e.g., "develop an interest in lifelong learning," "show a love for the discipline," "demonstrate critical thinking abilities"). Such broad goals violate the previous point, which was to make outcomes measurable. For an outcome to be measurable, it must be sufficiently concrete that criteria can be applied to distinguish higher from lower levels of performance. Students should have an idea of what the instructor's expectations are for a course as they read the learning outcomes. It might help to use action verbs, such as *identify, critique, compare and contrast, frame useful questions about . . ., identify the interaction between . . ., make decisions about . . . .*

Figure 3.3 in chapter 3 lists examples from three different disciplines as to how an instructor might start with a big idea, derive a few enduring understandings from it, and finally select a couple of relevant learning outcomes that match those understandings.

Step 4: Authentic Performance Tasks

As mentioned earlier, the foundation of meaningful learning outcomes needs both the link to the discipline's big ideas and enduring understandings, as well as to one or more authentic performance tasks. Students should not be assessed with relatively random tests and assignments, but with performance tasks that challenge them to demonstrate their true understanding of the key course concepts and ideas. Therefore, Steps 3 and 4 happen not consecutively, but in interaction with each other.

Performance tasks typically subsume multiple learning outcomes, and the performance criteria for these tasks as well as the key competencies cut across several outcomes. That implies that Step 4 still keeps the learning outcomes in mind as it creates one or more authentic performance tasks that serve learners as an entry point into the field. Students need to understand the types of problems and issues that an academic discipline addresses and how it applies its theoretical knowledge to realistic scenarios. The authentic performance task should address several learning outcomes in your course and should measure students' true understanding of key course concepts, theories, and procedures.

True understanding is hard to assess with multiple-choice questions on a test, and even the typical essay question often looks more for an intelligent summary of course content than for application of that knowledge to the real world. The best way to measure understanding is by requiring learners to work on a project that fulfills the following six criteria in order to be authentic. The task must: (1) be realistically contextualized, (2) require judgment and innovation, (3) ask the student to "do" the subject, (4) replicate key challenging situations in which professionals are truly "tested" in their field, (5) assess the student's ability to use a repertoire of knowledge and skill, and (6) allow appropriate opportunities to rehearse, practice, and get feedback.

This translates into a set of instructions that describes several key parameters of an authentic performance task, as one might outline a case study or a role play. They include a description of the larger *context* for the underlying problem, the *role* the student is to play in solving it, the actual *tasks* the student needs to perform, the final *product* to be submitted, and the person or persons who will be the clients and *assessors* of that final product. For examples of performance tasks in different disciplines, see chapter 6.

Step 5: Common Barriers and Misconceptions

The establishment of learning outcomes and related performance tasks now allows for the question: What systematic misconceptions are common as students approach a given task? Students enter college with many systematic barriers that jeopardize their accomplishment of the intended learning outcomes of the course. After years of experience with the student populations on their campus, faculty have developed a sense for what might cause the biggest barriers to students' conceptual understanding. Some barriers come from inadequate reasoning capabilities (e.g., identifying issues, assumptions, and implications in complex arguments). Others come from intellectual habits that get in the way of intellectual perseverance, awareness of own biases, tolerance for ambiguity, and so on. Particularly pertinent are the systematic misconceptions that students bring to key understandings in a discipline (e.g., overly simplistic models of how certain processes work in the natural sciences or stereotypes that preclude deeper understandings in the social sciences or humanities). Specific examples were provided in chapter 4.

Step 6: Essential Questions

Essential questions are designed to help students gain a deep, conceptual understanding of the course material. This often includes helping students address and overcome their learning barriers and misconceptions. It is therefore useful to phrase essential questions in close connection with common misconceptions.

Essential questions are the scaffold of the course. They cause relevant inquiry into the big ideas and core content, they require students to consider alternatives and justify their answers, they stimulate ongoing rethinking of prior lessons, and they create opportunities of transfer to other situations and subjects (see examples in chapter 5). An effective course is built as a continuum of questions that help learners unpack the meaning of the course content for themselves. Essential questions are therefore a good alternative to the daily or weekly course topics that make up the content list of a traditional syllabus. Each semester week should be guided by approximately 1 to 3 such questions.

Step 7: Guiding Concepts

Given your course's placement within the curriculum, what are the main concepts that your students should understand in order to address the course's essential questions? Concepts should not be confused with facts or topics. Topics are course-specific, whereas concepts transfer across course segments, across whole courses, and often also across disciplines (especially "macro-concepts" such as system, pattern, function, perspective, etc.). Concepts are the link between the course content and the enduring understandings and big ideas (see examples in chapter 5). Some concepts might fit under multiple learning outcomes, but the instructor should be clear on when each concept is first introduced to the students. That's the point at which they should be listed in the course design document. Confine yourself to listing only the key concepts of the course that probably every instructor could agree on, approximately 4 to 8 under each learning outcome.

Step 8: Task Performance Criteria

Complex performance tasks need to be assessed with sets of predefined criteria if grading is to be fair and students are to know exactly what is expected of them as they work on an assignment. Performance criteria break instructor expectations into several dimensions of quality that the students are expected to address. For example, if the task is to conduct a piece of research, the quality of that research depends on aspects such as identifying an appropriate issue or question, recognizing contextual factors that play a role, using appropriate data-collection procedures, and coming up with conclusions that are justifiable by the evidence collected. The total number of criteria for a given task depends on the complexity of that task, but should never get so big that students become confused about the subtle distinctions among the different criteria. Students are guided by these criteria, and they might need opportunities to practice following them before they do the real task. Setting up performance criteria is an intermediate step that helps with the final step, in which the instructor dissects which key competencies students need to have or develop in order to meet each given criterion. For more information, see chapter 7.

Step 9: Key Competencies

This step is often neglected in traditional course design. Instructors might assume that they recognize relevant deficits while they interact with students and can address those deficits as they emerge. But there is rarely any systematic, upfront planning for building in special time that allows students to work on shortcomings that need more than just a passing admonition by the instructor.

Given their explicit demands, the quality criteria for an authentic performance task are good guideposts for determining the key competencies that students need to successfully complete this task and demonstrate achievement of course learning outcomes. Students often fail on a task because they miss or are ill-prepared for an important step in the process. Experienced teachers can anticipate their students' stumbling blocks and break complex tasks into smaller components. For example, students might lack experience uncovering the underlying assumptions of a theory, considering the different perspectives that people from other cultures bring to an issue, or asking the right questions when doing a library search on a particular topic. The faculty member should be aware of the competencies that are critical but often lacking and design appropriate practice opportunities for students before they attack a major performance task of the course. See chapter 8.

Sample Course Design Document: Psychology 624—Theories of Motivation

Figures 9.1 and 9.2 show the complete course design document for the Psychology course Theories of Motivation that I have referred to in the previous chapters. Note that the figures do not completely follow the sequence of the nine steps just described. Step 4, the authentic performance task, is positioned at the beginning of figure 9.2 in order to allow the connection between learning outcomes, misconceptions, and essential questions in figure 9.1 to become more obvious. Figure 9.2 then illustrates the direct links between authentic performance tasks, performance criteria, and competencies.

I have included a blank course design document template (figure 9.3) to illustrate how the learning outcomes are nested within big ideas and enduring understandings, and how the other elements of figure 9.1 are grouped within the learning outcomes. This format reveals curricular alignment at a level not otherwise possible.

The first three columns in figure 9.1 show how the learning outcomes were derived from the enduring understandings, which, in turn, were generated from the discipline's big ideas. The next two columns, misconceptions and essential questions, look more toward the students and the horizons they bring to the course. Designing these two steps requires the instructor's awareness of the "logic of learning the content," as Wiggins and McTighe (2005) have called it. It takes into account that students are not empty slates, because they approach the class with their own conceptions, and those conceptions are important for framing the course content. The guiding concepts in the last column are influenced by the discipline as well as the students' learning barriers and the essential questions that are designed to help students overcome these barriers.

The second part of the course design document (figure 9.2) focuses on the performance tasks used in this course. The learning outcomes addressed by the performance task are cross-referenced. Each task is followed by the main criteria (as a rubric would define them) that apply to these tasks and the most relevant competencies that students need in order to do well on the task. In this case, the course has only one authentic performance task with five parts that address most of the learning outcomes. Note that instead of a single performance task, there could also be several smaller ones relating to maybe just one or two learning outcomes each. The large performance task outlined in figure 9.2 happens to address all learning outcomes, but additional smaller tasks could supplement the assessment of learning outcomes that are only partially addressed with the research project, such as outcomes 1, 5, and 6. A detailed description of the performance task is provided in figure 9.2. Figure 9.4 provides an example of an authentic performance task.

Summary of Course Design Features and Benefits

The course design document has a number of advantages over the traditional course syllabus. These features make it a unique tool for conceptualizing the framework for a course so that its essence can easily be communicated among instructors across sections, the curriculum, and even disciplines. The course design document identifies the crucial elements of a course that all instructors who teach sections of it should incorporate into their versions of the course. It thereby also defines the dimensions in which flexibility from instructor to instructor is perfectly appropriate.

More specifically, the course design document:

1. Makes learning outcomes meaningful by contextualizing them within the discipline and the larger curriculum. The proposed procedures don't just pick outcomes that feel right, but derive them from the big ideas and enduring understandings that define the field.
2. Brings coherence to backward design by fitting most components under enduring understanding and learning outcomes. Common barriers, essential questions, and guiding concepts are specified after proper learning outcomes have been established. Even performance tasks and key competencies are clearly determined in relation to the course outcomes.
3. Identifies nine key course dimensions that provide structure to teaching. Traditional course design only considers outcomes, content topics, and tests/assignments to provide a loose structure to a course. The course design document provides a whole toolbox for building a systematic scaffold on which to attach instructional activities.
4. Defines a course conceptually rather than through content. The main concern is what is necessary for students' deep understanding, not just what it is that they need to know.

FIGURE 9.4
The Authentic Performance Task for Psych. 624

The following is a detailed description of the main assignment for this course. It involves a research project that unfolds in several phases over 10 weeks of the semester. You have several options to choose from and can even come up with your own project, as long as I approve it. The next paragraphs describe the general format and procedure for this assignment, no matter which specific project you choose.

CONTEXT: We have an aging population in the United States, with large proportions of people living decades past retirement age. Many of them find themselves in various types of retirement communities. Many retirees seem to enjoy the relatively carefree state this stage of their lives provides; others feel bored and increasingly isolated from the rest of society. Issues such as changing self-concept, decreasing family ties, lack of challenge and opportunities for achievement, pessimism, and other aspects of motivation and emotion come into play in this environment. What can be done to keep the members of such retirement communities engaged and meaningfully challenged?

ROLE: You are a gerontologist who has been hired as a consultant by the director of the _____ retirement community to look into the mental health of the members of this community. You are given 10 weeks to complete your investigation and deliver your report.

TASK: You start by getting a general impression of the community. That implies questions such as: Which activities do the retirees engage in? Which seniors seem happier than others? What factors seem to play a major role in these discrepancies? You also want to talk with a few carefully selected members of the community and conduct interviews with both the seniors and staff. These interviews should gently probe into some of the issues mentioned under "context" above. The analysis of your observations and interviews should result in concrete recommendations about what works well in the community and what aspects of community life might need improvement.

PRODUCT: Your final report is to be given in two formats: (1) a paper that is handed in to your instructor for review and (2) a 10-minute presentation to the director (or other management staff) of the retirement community. The presentation may be either given in class with the director present, or via live or recorded video presented to the director.

ASSESSOR: Although the course instructor is the main assessor of the project, who will ultimately assign a final grade (based on the attached grading rubric), the director of the retirement community will also provide feedback to the student either orally or in writing. That feedback will indicate the practical usefulness of the student's report and the likelihood that any of the recommendations might be implemented in the future.

Below find three additional format options for a similar task from a different context. If you have a preference for another context, to which you have access, talk to me.

- You are a school psychologist who has been asked to investigate the trials and tribulations of being a senior at _____ High School. Your report should include observations regarding questions such as: Is the senior year in high school a lost time for education? Are students still intellectually engaged and challenged? You should include recommendations for improvement.
- You are a sports psychologist working with the local _____ team. The team has gone through some rough times lately and needs some insight into what has gone wrong and what can be done to motivate players (and staff) to turn things around.
- You are an industrial and organizational psychologist who has been called upon to consult on the dwindling numbers of volunteer workers in a local charitable organization. Your task is to find out what motivates the current volunteers to donate their time to the organization, as well as what turns them off. Your insight and recommendations are to be used to give more compelling arguments in the organization's recruitment efforts.

---

5. Identifies learning barriers for the student population by taking into account student characteristics (intellectual histories and belief structures) that create specific barriers for understanding. This goes significantly beyond just looking for features such as diverse learning styles or demographic differences of age, gender, ethnicity, and the like.

These benefits of the course design document are directly related to the advantages that idea-based course design has over content-based course design. Figure 9.5 provides a side-by-side comparison.

The course design document is a blueprint of the course structure, not a map for sequencing activities in the course, like the topics in a syllabus are used to build a logical progression from one week to the next. However, the "essential questions" help with creating a weekly outline for a course that is concerned with what students might find puzzling or counterintuitive to their preconceived notions about the course content.

Faculty still maintain considerable flexibility in how each one of them teaches a version of a given course. For a course to have a recognizable identity, it is necessary for its sections to have the same set of learning outcomes and derivations from big ideas and enduring understandings. It is also important that it has a minimal set of identical guiding concepts. Beyond that, the elements may vary somewhat. Faulty thinking and essential questions might take on a different slant for different student populations. Performance tasks, related criteria, and key competencies could vary even more

FIGURE 9.5
Advantages of Idea-Based Course Design

	Content-Based	Idea-Based
Organized around:	Topics and facts	Big ideas, enduring understandings, and essential questions (funnel)
Evidence of learning:	Tests and decontextualized assignments	(Mostly) authentic performance tasks
Purpose of assessment:	Summative evaluation (in order to assign grades)	Formative assessment that provides frequent practice and feedback opportunities
Function of the syllabus:	Contract with punitive undertones	Sense-making tool for periodic reflection and discussion
Assessment criteria:	Instructor-owned and rarely shared in any detail	Teaching tool that is shared with students for practicing purposes
Link to curriculum:	Usually implicit and hardly ever made explicit	Task for active reflection
Curricular alignment:	Claimed, but cannot be demonstrated	All nine course elements are clearly interconnected
Critical thinking:	Hoped-for but not purposefully pursued	Integrated by systematically addressing students' misconceptions
Faculty role:	Imparting knowledge	Coaching for learning
Student role:	Receiving knowledge—largely passively	Actively making sense of the larger conceptual framework

from class section to section, not to mention teaching style and daily classroom activities.

It is important, though, to create a complete course design document that is considered the master plan for all sections. The clarity and discipline it provides in outlining what needs to be accomplished during the semester should not be traded for rigid insistence on flexibility and academic autonomy. Integrity of the curriculum and transparent and coherent planning for student learning come first.

Translating the Course Design Document Into a Syllabus

The course design document is for the benefit of faculty and administrators. Does this mean that the students won't get to see any of the planning that went into this document in the syllabus they receive? Certainly not. Syllabi can be modified to include key elements from the course design document to help students develop a better understanding of the overall framework of the course. The appendix illustrates what such a syllabus might look like for the Theories of Motivation course. Here is a short description of eight special features that can be added to the traditional syllabus to communicate in a learning-centered fashion (see Grunert O'Brien et al., *The Course Syllabus*, 2008) the instructor's course design.

- Description of Big Ideas
  The short course descriptions in the traditional class catalogues are usually not very informative. Adding brief outlines of the big ideas underlying the course would improve students' conceptual understanding of the course purpose.
- Concept Map of Big Ideas, Enduring Understanding, and Learning Outcomes
  Linda Nilson (2007) has advocated the "graphic syllabus" to visually illustrate the course organization. I believe that at least the derivation of the learning outcomes for the course can be clearly represented in a concept map that is particularly useful for our visually oriented students. Free software for creating concept maps is available on the Web.
- The Recurring Activities in the Course (Course Modules)
  Online courses in particular tend to be organized in modules, that is, segments of one or more weeks that follow the same format of activities. The example in the appendix adapts this approach to a face-to-face course.
- The Authentic Performance Task
  The main course project is an authentic performance task that is explained in detail under the subheadings *context, role, task, product,* and *assessor.*
- Performance Criteria for That Task
  The course project is divided into five different sub-assignments, each of which has a set of three or four criteria that are relevant for this part of the assignment.

- Student Collaboration for Completing Grading Rubrics
  All the parts of the assignment might not require a full-blown grading rubric. The ones that do (in our example, the last two parts) will benefit from students helping to turn the sets of performance criteria into complete rubrics.
- Week-by-Week Sequence of Essential Questions
  The last part of the syllabus is a week-by-week outline of the course. Instead of using chapter headings from the reading assignments, this outline provides a more conceptual overview of the course that lists the essential questions that the course addresses.
- Student Reflections About Key Course Elements
  Once the course syllabus contains all this information about the course rationale, the syllabus itself can become a learning tool. Students are asked for short reflections about key elements of the course at three strategically selected times in the semester.

KNOWLEDGE ROOMS IN AN ONLINE COURSE

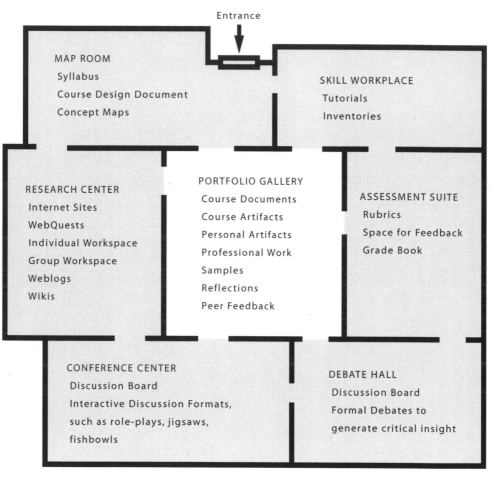

Entrance

MAP ROOM
Syllabus
Course Design Document
Concept Maps

SKILL WORKPLACE
Tutorials
Inventories

RESEARCH CENTER
Internet Sites
WebQuests
Individual Workspace
Group Workspace
Weblogs
Wikis

PORTFOLIO GALLERY
Course Documents
Course Artifacts
Personal Artifacts
Professional Work
Samples
Reflections
Peer Feedback

ASSESSMENT SUITE
Rubrics
Space for Feedback
Grade Book

CONFERENCE CENTER
Discussion Board
Interactive Discussion Formats,
such as role-plays, jigsaws,
fishbowls

DEBATE HALL
Discussion Board
Formal Debates to
generate critical insight

IO

IMPLEMENTING COURSE
DESIGN WITH ONLINE
TECHNOLOGY

OVERVIEW

KEY CHARACTERISTICS OF ONLINE TEACHING

COURSE DESIGN ELEMENTS ENHANCED BY ONLINE TECHNOLOGY

- Essential questions
- Guiding concepts for the course
- Common learning barriers
- Authentic performance tasks
- Rubrics
- Key competencies and practice opportunities
- Learning outcomes and big ideas

CONCLUSION

This book ends with a look at how the idea-based course design format can be implemented with online technology. Why online technology? Designing a course for online delivery—even partial online delivery—demands a certain amount of discipline that is beneficial to the course design process in general. It compels us to be more structured and purposeful in our planning than face-to-face courses tend to do. Face-to-face courses tempt us to postpone some decisions and finalize the course once it has already started to unfold. Leaving some decisions to be made after we have gotten to know the students in the class bears some logic, but there is a danger of being less than systematic about how it all fits together. Planning an online course requires the instructor to make every part of the course design explicit and coherent, and to do so ahead of the semester. That type of rigor fosters a course design where all the pieces fit together. In addition, there are some characteristics of online teaching that can improve the students' learning experience in unexpected ways.

Key Characteristics of Online Teaching

This chapter will make the case that the principles of idea-based course design can be implemented particularly well with online tools and strategies commonly embraced by hybrid and online teaching. Teaching online has some undeniable characteristics that set it apart from face-to-face instruction, and those characteristics can be used to considerable advantage. Five such critical features come to mind:

1. *Integration of media:*
   The Internet represents the integration of all media: text-based, video, and audio. All of these media can be used synchronously and asynchronously for either live or delayed communication. In addition, because the Internet is not merely a learning tool but also a tool used for business, news broadcasts, publishing, entertainment, and so on, it allows online learning to interface seamlessly with these other functions and to connect the virtual classroom directly with the real world. This changes the nature of the classroom, allowing students to interact with other audiences in addition to their instructor, thereby giving them a potentially more authentic learning experience.
2. *Conscious community:*
   In a face-to-face class, every student automatically has a social presence by virtue of taking up physical space, even if they remain quiet

throughout the whole semester. In an online course, students need to establish a presence by interacting with the technology and with other members of the course. In order for an online course to become an effective learning environment, students (and instructors) have to explicitly negotiate the norms and goals for collaborating with each other. Face-to-face classes tend to fall back on long-held, tacit expectations about classroom interaction. Online courses succeed only through the creation of a learning community that gives every class member an incentive for participating in and contributing to a common purpose. Without this synergy, an online course is nothing but a collection of text messages (see Palloff & Pratt, 2007).

3. *Electronic class history:*
Everything that happens in an online course is documented for everyone to see, if so desired. All contributions to the classroom discourse are stored in files, and the instructor and students can go back to these contributions to evaluate what was said by whom. There can be no controversy over the nature of any student's participation in the class. At the same time, all these stored contributions represent their own body of class content, which might be a valuable part of the course content itself. Students thereby become not just participants but also coauthors of the course.

4. *Comprehensive review:*
This electronic class history makes it possible for students to do a comprehensive review of what has been said in class at any point during the semester. They can, therefore, be more easily held responsible for the material of the entire course, not just the most recent chapters since the last test. Face-to-face courses have a much harder time revisiting what was learned in the early parts of the course and synthesizing material over the whole stretch of the semester.

5. *Detailed diagnostics and tutoring:*
One thing computers do very well is to help break down tasks into small steps. Students can review these steps as often as they want, and instructors can diagnose the exact spot where students fail to understand, build in different ways of explaining difficult concepts or procedures, and keep track of students' progress as they grapple with the material. Properly designed computer programs (tutorials, simulations, etc.) are, therefore, the perfect tool to help students practice and to assess the skills minutiae they have or have not yet learned.

These five characteristics of online teaching happen to be closely related to key features of the course design format described in the previous chapters. The course design document presented in chapter 9 can serve as a framework that is particularly useful for online courses. In turn, the various elements that make up this document also benefit greatly from the online medium and its qualities of supporting authentic tasks that transcend the classroom, place a premium on detail-oriented practice and feedback, and support activities for repeated review and deep understanding of main concepts and ideas. In fact, the course design elements described in this book can serve as the building blocks for effective online courses. This list includes:

Content and Skills:
1. Essential questions that guide students into the core content
2. The guiding concepts for the course
3. Common barriers that students encounter in trying to understand course concepts or in trying to acquire course skills

Assessment:
4. Authentic performance tasks challenging students to demonstrate their understanding in meaningful contexts
5. Task criteria (rubrics) that measure students' performance
6. Key abilities that students must have in order to satisfy those criteria, as well as practice opportunities for acquiring these abilities
7. Learning outcomes, as derived from big ideas and enduring understandings, providing the framework for student assessment

One other critical feature that distinguishes online courses from face-to-face ones is the fact that, in some regard, online courses are physical spaces rather than temporal events. Whereas in an on-campus course the teaching and learning happen in a linear fashion as the synchronous interactions unfold, the online course has its material all laid out before the students enter. Some researchers, like Van B. Weigel (2002) and Linda Harasim (1990), prefer to use the analogy of different physical spaces that students enter as they engage different tasks and activities of the course. Weigel defines seven different spaces ("knowledge rooms") that provide a visual way of distinguishing the different types of learning (or the different aspects of the class) that might take place in an online course:

Research Center
This is a place in which students conduct (or deposit) their inquiry activities for the course. For example, students might work in small groups on a class project that will later be presented to the whole group.

Skill Workplace

This part of the course provides students with opportunities to practice and acquire key skills necessary for understanding course content and performing more complex assignments. For example, students might go through a number of tutorials related to specific concepts or procedures in the field.

Conference Center

This center is designed for students to reflect on important issues and communicate with each other in an effort to gain a deeper understanding and possibly resolve problems that the course material presents. Electronic forums with threaded discussions are common examples of what might be found in the conference center.

Debate Hall

This place represents a more formal version of the conference center. Instead of merely exploring certain issues in collaborative discussion, the debate hall has students (or teams of students) test prepared arguments in formal debate.

Portfolio Gallery

As the term *gallery* indicates, students present their work here for the review and feedback of their fellow students, their instructor, and possibly non-class members.

Assessment Suite

This area includes secure spaces for performance reviews and grade reports to individual students. It also houses the criteria (or rubrics) for evaluating student performance, as well as self-assessment forms to help students rate their performance on their own.

Map Room

Given the complexity of a fully developed online course, it is always possible for students to become disoriented; the map room includes tools to prevent this from happening. The syllabus and other navigational resources are available, together with an advising and student feedback space, student and instructor bios, and so on.

The image of an online course as a suite of virtual spaces helps students understand how the different course activities supplement each other and support student learning. Students can recognize the value of the different learning tools in each of the knowledge rooms (see Chapter 10 Graph). This encourages them, for example, to spend time in the Skill Workplace and maybe the Conference Center or the Debate Hall before engaging a project in the Research Center and finally exhibiting it in the Portfolio Gallery, all the while paying intermittent visits to the Assessment Suite for formative feedback. Instructors, too, will find it useful to present the learning process in those terms and to be able to trace whether a student has followed such routes or taken shortcuts.

Course Design Elements Enhanced by Online Technology

After this excursion into some of the unique features of online learning, we are now ready to look at the course design elements one by one and explore how online environments can be structured around them. We will start with the elements that are most closely related to the course content—essential questions, key concepts, and common barriers—and then move to those elements that determine students' assessment in the course—authentic performance tasks, rubrics, key competencies and related practice opportunities, and the learning outcomes that hold them all together.

Essential Questions

Essential questions provide the skeleton for the course content. They present the main issues each course module needs to address and also allow for connections between the conceptual ideas of the course. Face-to-face courses use class discussions to help students gain a deeper understanding of the subtleties and competing perspectives involved in complex issues. Online courses mimic this format by using electronic discussion forums that allow for a proper exchange of opinions and arguments, and they compensate for a lack in spontaneity with reflection and careful wording. An additional benefit of the online medium is that virtually all students get to participate in the discussion, while face-to-face discussions are often dominated by a small group of outspoken students. The virtual space in which these discussions happen is aptly described by Weigel's term "conference center." It has its own electronic tools (the electronic discussion board) and its own rules of organized group discourse.

Simple discussion forums are not the only format for addressing essential questions in an online course. Rena Palloff and Keith Pratt (2005) describe in detail a number of formats that get students to engage with the issues and with each other; five of them are briefly summarized in figure 10.1. All of them take advantage of the strengths of the asynchronous medium for slowing down the rapid back-and-forth that characterizes live interaction. This allows participants to be more deliberate in their contributions by drafting their responses in writing and posting them at the appropriate moment. It becomes easier to practice taking a leadership role in a discussion when there is time to consider one's next move before acting. Verbal interactions that are documented in text can be used for careful debriefing, and self- as well as peer-assessment become common features of online activities.

Guiding Concepts for the Course

The emphasis of idea-based course design is on conceptual understanding. As described in chapter 5, guiding concepts are preferable over knowledge-based course topics for providing students with an entry into the workings of the discipline. Guiding concepts can be rather short-lived in face-to-face courses. Textbooks boldface them and list them in their index. The instructor might add them to a handout for test preview. It can be a challenge to constantly keep them in the forefront of students' minds as the course progresses.

In online courses, guiding concepts can maintain an ongoing presence. They should be listed in what Weigel calls the "map room," where they can be revisited easily as the course requires it. There are different ways of storing guiding concepts in the map room. The instructor might have students collaborate on a wiki that allows them to update their understanding of each concept as the course progresses and new meanings and relationships between guiding concepts become visible. *PsychWiki* (Stenstrom & Iyer, 2010), a tool for psychologists, is a good example for how this works. In this case, anybody on the World Wide Web—not just a particular college classroom—can edit, correct, or update the information contained in articles under broad psychological categories or subdisciplines, such as cognition, motivation, personality, the self, and the like. Wikis can be created for any size-context: for self-contained courses, for courses that open their doors to other courses on campus or beyond, and for the whole Internet community. It is easy to see how such a tool could keep the discussion of guiding course concepts fresh and ongoing throughout the semester or even over consecutive versions of the same course, semester after semester.

Another useful online tool for organizing course concepts is the concept map. The concept mapping technique was developed in the 1960s at Cornell

FIGURE 10.1
Interactive Discussion Formats

Role-Playing

In groups that comprise the different stakeholders/roles in a scenario, individual students research the position their respective role is likely to embody. Each player writes an essay establishing and supporting this position and shares that essay with the group. Each student then posts comments on the essays of at least two other students on the team. A final self-assessment requires each player to state what they learned by playing the role and what they learned about the process as a whole.

Dyads

Students either select a partner or are assigned one by the instructor. Both research a course-related issue or problem of interest to them. They then post the results of their collaboration to the discussion board. This post might include suggestions for how to address the problem, what changes they propose, and what strategies they intend to use in implementing these changes. Self- and peer-assessment should follow.

Jigsaw Activities

These are a good way to expand the content presented in an online course by asking learners to become experts in an area and to present that area to their peers. The instructor might provide a list of topics that are related to (a portion of) the course. Individual students then explore one topic and present their findings to the class. Members of the class then have the opportunity to engage in discussion with the author of each paper for a certain period of time, for example, one week.

Debates

The instructor sets up the debate around a topic that is just controversial enough to allow students to take a position but not so controversial that it might result in personal attacks. Rules and guidelines for debate are established in advance. Students have a choice to take the *pro* or *con* position on the issue. They write a one-to-two page statement outlining (a) the background to the debate, (b) major arguments in support of their position, and (c) answers to challenges expected from the opposing position. Students respond to one or two learners with whom they disagree and engage in a mini-debate in which they exchange at least three ideas. Following the debate, each student prepares a final post, indicating whether or not their position has changed and noting why and how.

Fishbowls

Small groups sign up to facilitate and discuss the content of special units of the course. Each group member is expected to facilitate one day while the remainder of the group participates in the discussion. The rest of the class functions as observers of the process, taking notes and reflecting on the performance of the group in the fishbowl. The last day of each discussion week is a debriefing session for all learners.

(Palloff and Pratt, 2005)

University by Joseph D. Novak, who, together with his colleague Alberto Cañas, updated his original theory for concept maps in a 2006 report. In this report, the authors also describe *Cmap,* one of several free concept-mapping software tools. *Cmap* does online what used to be simple paper-and-pencil balloons, connected with straight lines and marked with appropriate labels that identify each concept and the nature of its relationship with surrounding concepts. Being an online tool, *Cmap* can do considerably more than its paper-and-pencil counterparts. It can link resources such as photos, graphs, videos, and whole Web pages, to any concept bubble on the map, and it also allows adding discussion threads and annotations in the form of Post-Its. Individual students can develop their own concept maps, or groups of students may work on a collaborative concept map. In either case, guiding course concepts play a very different role from the boldfaced and indexed print definitions of concepts in textbooks.

Common Learning Barriers

Chapter 4 examined four barriers to learning and critical thinking: intellectual development, habits of mind, misconceptions, and complex reasoning. Online tools and procedures can help learners overcome some of these. In some respects, the easier barriers to address deal with cognitive issues, because students don't have to develop insight into their own psychological shortcomings before they can see improvement. Cognitive barriers are the content of most textbooks on critical thinking and complex reasoning. They deal with issues of formal logic, including validity, logical fallacies, formats of argumentation, and other questionable uses of language. The Internet is full of lessons and even interactive tutorials that address these hurdles. Some examples include:

- Humboldt State University's Argumentation and Critical Thinking Tutorial: www.humboldt.edu/~act/HTML/tests.html
- The Training Place's Online Resources and Tutorials for Successful Intentional Learning or Distance Learning: www.trainingplace.com/loq/strategies.htm
- The Institute for Teaching and Learning's "Mission: Critical" Web page at San Jose State University: www.sjsu.edu/depts/itl/
- Joe Lau and Jonathan Chan from the University of Hong Kong's Critical Thinking web site: http://philosophy.hku.hk/think/

In addition to these free tools, commercial tools, such as Pearson's *MySkillsLab* or *MyLogicLab* are also available. Commercial tools usually have the advantage of being more comprehensive and consistently supported by the company that markets them. They also generate assessment data that can be downloaded into course-management systems for use in grading and program evaluation. Both the free and commercial tools are conveniently integrated into an online course and provide the advantage of allowing students to practice these skills repeatedly and in great detail over the course of the semester. Face-to-face courses can hardly afford the time for students to go through extended drill-and-practice sequences in class, and conventional paper-and-pencil assignments tend to be much less engaging for students.

Unfortunately, drill-and-practice activities rarely remove barriers that are created by students' naive dualistic worldviews, by counterproductive intellectual habits of mind, or by deeply ingrained misconceptions of complex phenomena. These barriers require students to broaden their horizons and confront their own intellectual shortcomings. Such confrontations can be initiated with self-inventories that assess learning styles (VARK Questionnaire), multiple intelligences (MI-Inventory), and intellectual development. For a selection of these, see the Association of American Colleges and Universities' listing (2010). Bear in mind that the results of these inventories will require further reflection, discussion, and carefully directed class debate to generate the critical insight that students need to develop about themselves. Weigel's "debate hall" provides a context that keeps such debates separate from the discussions in the "conference center," where different, legitimate perspectives on issues are exchanged. The debates on student misconceptions require more than an exchange of opinions; they need to result in a fundamental change of mind. Joan Davis (2009) refers to a few electronic tools that seem to help further with conceptual change of students' misconceptions:

> *Concept Mapping* has already been mentioned in the previous section. Concept maps allow instructors to see the types of connections that students make or fail to make. They also allow students to see how their conceptions change over time and thereby become instrumental in helping students confront inconsistencies in their belief systems.
>
> *Constructing History: How Historians See the Light* (Library of Congress, 2000) is an example of a tutorial that demonstrates why history is not—as many students believe—a body of factual knowledge that is not subject to interpretation. It shows how the nature of historical sources requires judgment and is always open to controversy.
>
> *The Web-Based Inquiry Science Environment (WISE)* is another example of how online tutorials and simulations can help students understand why it

is often difficult for scientists to agree on one answer. In *WISE,* students work on inquiry projects for topics such as global climate change and population genetics, and respond to scientific controversies by designing, debating, and critiquing solutions. Similar simulation programs are available in MERLOT (www.merlot.org).

Authentic Performance Tasks

Chapter 8 emphasized the importance of "assignment-centered" instruction and the role of "authentic performance tasks," which confront students with the types of problems and issues that an academic discipline addresses and require the application of its theoretical knowledge to realistic scenarios. They thereby make it possible to assess students' true understanding of key course concepts, theories, and procedures. Offering authentic, real-world tasks is one of the greatest strengths of online courses, because each online course is automatically connected with the World Wide Web, which literally opens the world for students to explore. Until the arrival of the Internet, it was very cumbersome for courses to build real-life tasks into the curriculum. Now the Internet provides a seamless connection between what students do in the virtual classroom and the real-world resources and situations that are just one mouse click away.

In his book *The World Is Open* (2009), Curt Bonk describes a variety of data-rich environments that can serve as resources for authentic assignments. These include online museums, such as the National Museum of African American History and Culture; the British Library, which is digitizing the actual works of da Vinci, Jane Austen, Mozart, and others; Cambridge University's "Complete Works of Charles Darwin Online"; the "Einstein Archives Online"; "Exploring and Collecting History Online"; the Public Library of Science, with freely available scientific and medical literature; and, of course, the Museum of Online Museums.

Authentic performance tasks employ the types of scenarios that are also used in problem-based learning. The University of Delaware maintains a Clearinghouse for Problem-Based Learning, with nearly 150 case-based activities that faculty have submitted from their own classroom experience. Figure 10.2 describes just a few of these scenarios. Go to http://primus.nss.udel.edu/Pbl/ for more detail.

Another way of allowing students to work on tasks that come fairly close to real-world problems are WebQuests. These are guided Web assignments that require students to explore a number of Web resources—usually

FIGURE 10.2
Problem-Based Learning Assignments From the Problem-Based Learning Clearinghouse

BIOLOGY
Roots: Exploring Our Distant Ancestry

Although most students take a position for or against evolution, few actually understand the concept of natural selection or appreciate the idea of descent with modification. This activity challenges students to provide structured arguments and evidence for their belief-based conclusions on either side of the creation–evolution issue. The "right answer" is insufficient without support. The problem focuses on characteristics of human ancestors (e.g., scales) rather than the ancestors themselves (e.g., fish or reptiles), requires students to use the library/ Internet resources, and gives them practice with oral and written communication.

EDUCATION
Choosing Books to Support Elementary Girls' Science Learning

In this problem designed for teacher education majors, students prepare a grant proposal to obtain trade books for elementary science curricula that will support girls' science learning. Students will first determine what makes a good science trade book for children, examine books within a particular content area for their quality and appeal to girls, determine a list of text materials appropriate for instruction, and prepare a grant application to request those materials.

ENGLISH
A Case for the Classics

Non-English majors often perceive literary study as perfunctory to their "real" career goals. These attitudes can become a hurdle, especially in a literature course that includes texts representing a time and setting that are unfamiliar to contemporary students. This problem, emphasizing collaborative work, asks students to explore within these not-so-contemporary texts, elements that make them examples of demonstrably enduring quality. The problem evokes an exploration of texts, which requires students to explore the texts in an effort to uncover how they are a product of setting and society at a certain point in sociocultural history, yet represent elements that make them valuable in contemporary times. The students are challenged to think beyond the text and make connections with other texts and contemporary life.

ENERGY AND ENVIRONMENTAL POLICY
The First 100 Days: Energy Policy and the U.S. President's Administration

In this problem, multidisciplinary teams are asked to assume the role of experts in energy policy and make a recommendation for the new U.S. president's administration to take action in its first 100 days. Teams are to seek vigorous approaches for reducing carbon dioxide emissions by seven billion tons per year. Students prepare a white paper on their findings, with corresponding budget and scientific detail, and defend their recommendations in a 20-minute presentation to a team of local experts playing the role of congressmen.

MEDICAL EDUCATION
To Resuscitate or Not to Resuscitate

Patients' rights are a basic value in health care. Adult patients of sound mind must be informed of their medical diagnosis, prognosis, treatment options, and the pros and cons of those options. The adult patient of sound mind should determine, in conjunction with their health care practitioner, their course of medical treatment. At times, the patients' values and desires for treatment are contrary to the health care practitioners' values. The health care practitioner might have a different opinion or preferred treatment than what the patient wishes. Several rules and documents have been put into place to help ensure the patients' wishes are carried out. This case is an example of how the different wishes of the patient and health care practitioner can come into conflict.

POLITICAL SCIENCE
Alleviating the AIDS Crisis in South Africa

South Africa, along with several other southern African countries, has among the highest HIV infection rates in the world. This problem examines some of the implications of the AIDS epidemic in South Africa and the possible approaches to alleviating it. The problem also addresses issues concerning bilateral relations between developed and developing countries, and the role of multinational corporations and multilateral institutions in world politics.

---

preselected by the instructor—to help them experience what it would be like to execute a project in their future profession. WebQuests can be and have been created in virtually any discipline. A few examples include:

- History: *Life During the Great Depression—Time Capsule*
  Students research the lives of people during this period and collect artifacts in the form of primary sources to include in a time capsule about the Great Depression.
- Education: *Technology Meets Multiple Intelligences*
  Expands students' knowledge of Howard Gardner's theory of multiple intelligences and provides resources for integrating it with the use of classroom technologies
- Education: *Web 2.0 in the Classroom: An Educational Odyssey*
  Students learn how to make blogs, wikis, podcasts, complex Power-Points, and movies, while they are designing a problem-based learning unit for a class of their choosing.
- Biology: *Epidemic Investigation*
  Given sets of geographically mapped data, students need to decide whether a mysterious illness in California should be classified as an epidemic.

- Business: *International Transaction Analysis*
  Students research costs and legal requirements associated with importing a product, use the information to analyze the transaction, and recommend for or against importing the product.

Go to San Diego State University's WebQuest Web page at http://web quest.org/index.php to find about 2,500 more such examples. Students collaborate or work alone on these tasks that typically take considerable time to complete. Outcomes are presented in a variety of formats, from written reports and narrated PowerPoint presentations to wikis and Weblogs with embedded video and audio files.

Other types of assignments go even further in their effort to erase the division between the classroom and the real world. Michael Wesch, a cultural anthropologist at Kansas State University, has involved his students in the YouTube Ethnography Project, which explores the YouTube phenomenon. As a class assignment, each student in the course produced his or her own three- to five-minute video ethnography of some aspect of the YouTube community (see http://mediatedcultures.net/youtube.htm). Students' research products, the videos, were then posted on YouTube for further input from anybody willing to respond. Many other examples exist for class assignments that make use of the collaborative authoring capabilities of Web 2.0.

The types of projects described here under "authentic performance tasks" fit into what Weigel has called the "research center" within an online course. The research center gives individuals or groups of students specific resources for collecting, sharing, and analyzing information and preparing a summary of their work.

Rubrics

Rubrics are a key tool for self-assessment and performance feedback on competencies and tasks that are hard to quantify. Authentic performance tasks, online discussion forums, student portfolios, and the like, would be impossible to assess without the analytical components of a scoring rubric. Higher education has finally embraced them, although primarily as a tool for program assessment and accreditation. Websites have emerged (such as Rubrician.com or Kathy Schrock's Guide for Educators) that provide a wealth of examples for rubrics addressing a wide variety of purposes. There is even a site (Rubistar) that provides assistance with the development of rubrics, as well as a rubric to assess rubrics (www.idecorp.com). The Association of American Colleges and Universities created the Valid Assessment of Learning in Undergraduate Education project that developed fifteen rubrics covering core intellectual skills, competencies in personal and social responsibility as well as integrative and applied learning.

Online courses make it easy for students to be aware of the criteria that the instructor has created for judging the quality of their performance on a given assignment. Learning management systems, such as Blackboard and Epsilen, and e-portfolio software, such as LiveText, allow students to open up a window on the grading rubric for their current assignment anytime they enter their course. They can review their instructor's scoring and comments via that rubric together with the electronically returned assignment. With the rubric, they can also receive peer feedback in the same way or do a self-assessment before they hand in the assignment. Of equal importance is the ability for students and instructors alike to review previous assignments and observe changes in performance on specific dimensions of the rubric. E-portfolios (see "Learning Outcomes and Big Ideas") keep all these assessments organized—no more lost documents and loose-leaf binders that make any longitudinal performance review a chore.

Rubrics reside in multiple spaces of a virtual class. They might be attached to activities that are performed in Weigel's "skill workplace," in the "conference center," and certainly in the "assessment suite." But they are all individually displayed in the "map room," where students can examine, ahead of any given task, the criteria the instructor will use to evaluate their success on that task.

Key Competencies and Practice Opportunities

Once the instructor has identified the performance criteria for a complex task, she or he has to determine the competencies that students need to develop in order to meet those criteria. And once those competencies have been identified, students need opportunities to practice them. One of the basic strengths discovered in the early days of instructional computing was its ability to provide many variations of practice scenarios with instant supportive and nonjudgmental feedback. Computer-assisted instruction was the forerunner of today's sophisticated online tutorial, which not only provides practice and feedback sessions but also diagnoses students' level of mastery (see "Common Learning Barriers"), branches to appropriate difficulty levels, and keeps track of students' progress over time. Because these tools are seamlessly integrated into online courses, online teaching can provide a learning environment unmatched by face-to-face classes when it comes to drill and practice sessions. Few face-to-face courses can afford the practice time required of students, especially those marginally prepared, to learn the skills for performing increasingly complex tasks.

If students have serious academic deficits, complex tutoring systems, such as PLATO and Pearson's *MyLab* series might be required to bring students up to required levels. These commercial programs provide many hundreds of hours of programming and have the above-mentioned branching and tracking features built in. Noncommercial online tutorials and smaller learning objects are available on a number of different websites. They typically address select aspects of core skills (such as writing, critical thinking, and information literacy), or were designed for more specific tasks in almost any discipline. Figure 10.3 provides a few examples for what is available on the Internet free of charge.

The practice of competencies happens in Weigel's "skill workplace," where access may be provided to any number of tutorials, diagnostic inventories, and other job aids. Because skills typically also require some reflection, and possibly instructor or peer feedback, some of the students' skill training will also spill over into the "conference center" to help deepen the understanding that fosters further improvement.

Learning Outcomes and Big Ideas

Deriving learning outcomes from big ideas and enduring understandings typically constitutes the first step in course design (see chapter 3). These learning outcomes then become the guideposts for everything else that happens in a course, including student activities and assignments and their assessment. Unfortunately, they also tend to become largely invisible to students as the course progresses. Online courses provide a unique opportunity to keep intended outcomes visible throughout the term and to document the degree to which students accomplished those outcomes. This is because everything ever posted in an online course is preserved. Students can go back at any time to review what has been presented or discussed by any class member and reflect on how these contributions were linked (or not) to the intended learning outcomes of the course.

A research group for Penn State's e-portfolio system discovered that e-portfolios were initially ineffective because students were not quite aware of the relevance of the intended learning outcomes. They "didn't realize you were doing them until afterward . . ." or "didn't know it would be important to accomplish them" (PSU, 2009). This illustrates the advantage of starting

FIGURE 10.3
Skills Tutorials Online

Wisconsin Online—http://www.wisc-online.com
Tutorials for Core Skills on:

Critical Thinking, Written Communication, Speech Communication, Oral/Interpersonal Communication, Reading, Teamwork, Problem Solving, Attitude

BBC Skillswise—http://www.bbc.co.uk/skillswise
Tutorials for Core Skills on:

Grammar (adverbs, personal pronouns, verb–subject agreement, using commas, making sentences, putting sentences together); *Reading* (fact vs. opinion, types of text, scanning, summarizing, skimming); *Writing* (paragraphs, planning your writing, proofreading, format and structure, story writing)

MERLOT—http://www.merlot.org
Sample Tutorials for:

Information Literacy
  • *Find That Book!—Competitive Core Research Skills—21st Century Information Fluency Project Portal—Evaluating Internet Sources and Sites—Finding Articles—Publish Not Perish—Research It Right!—Searching the Web*

Business
  • *Mini-cases From Lockheed Martin*—A series of 20 interactive cases that concern ethical dilemmas in business
  • *Writing Skills for Tax Professionals*—Lessons on topics of "Tax Research Memos," "Writing Client Letters," and "The Judicial Brief" are followed by feedback-enabled self-tests
  • *Web Marketing Tutorial and Guide*—Includes topics like search engine optimization, search engine advertising, reciprocal link programs, site search, affiliate marketing programs
  • *Bookkeeping and Accounting Interactive Tutor*—Covers topics such as the "accounting equation," double entries, and accruals and prepayments

Education
  • *Authentic Assessment Toolbox*—A how-to hypertext on creating authentic tasks, rubrics, and standards for measuring and improving student learning
  • *Strategies for Assessing Learning Effectiveness*—This tutorial provides a set of exemplary strategies for assessing the effectiveness of different pedagogies and technologies based on current "best practices" within the field of educational research.
  • *Active Learning Practice for Schools (ALPS)*—ALPS is a tool and tutorial designed to help faculty understand what meaningful teaching and learning look like. Harvard Project Zero resources are provided to help teachers reflect on their teaching practice, brainstorm ideas, and design curriculum.

FIGURE 10.3 (Continued)

The Humanities
- *Guide to Grammar and Writing*—Everything from the basic parts of speech all the way to writing the argumentative essay and using proper MLA format
- *It's No Laughing Matter: Analyzing Political Cartoons*—How to analyze cartoons and persuasive techniques of political cartoonists to promote their individual message, such as symbolism, exaggeration, and analogy
- *The Difference Between Right and Wrong*—Explains key forms of normative judgments and fundamental divisions of normative theories
- *The Historian's Toolbox*—To start a beginning history student in topic selection, topic survey, and basic research strategies

The Social Sciences
- *Sampling in Social Research*—Explains the uses of probability sampling to students of introductory social research methods and demonstrates applications of various sampling strategies
- *Experimental Design: Internal Validity*—Introduces nine sources of threat to internal validity
- *Science and Race: Concept and Category*—Illustrates the meaning of "race" and how the concept evolved
- *Red States, Blue States: Electoral Strategy Behind the Map*—Enhances users' understanding of the 2008 U.S. presidential election, identifies patterns and trends that impact the election process, and explores different election scenarios with an interactive map

Math and Sciences
- *LabWrite: Improving Lab Reports*—Guides students through the entire lab experience, with resources divided into four parts that are structured around the lab process: PreLab, InLab, PostLab, and LabCheck
- *Virtual Chemistry Lab*—A chance to mix chemicals without wearing safety goggles; choose solutions from the vast database and mix them together till the cloned cows come home
- *PhET: Physics Education Technology at the University of Colorado*—Interactive, research-based simulations of physical phenomena from the PhET project at the University of Colorado
- *Mathematical Visualization Toolkit*—A collection of plotting and solving applets, featuring a uniform user interface

with a few big ideas and deriving enduring understandings from them before selecting appropriate learning outcomes that fit under these enduring understandings. The procedure provides critical context for students to truly understand what their learning outcomes mean and then use them as an organizing principle for the portfolio. If that is not enough, the essential questions that guide each course module provide yet another layer that students can use to organize their portfolio.

A number of different e-portfolio systems exist, and many of them have been designed to integrate with one or more of the leading course-management systems, including Blackboard, Desire2Learn, Sakai, Moodle, Epsilen, to name a few. This integration creates the perfect space for what Weigel has called a "portfolio gallery." Students exhibit work samples that might represent their best accomplishments in the course, or that illustrate their personal growth from beginning to semester end, or that document their insights into what they found worth learning in the course.

Some e-portfolio systems were mainly designed as assessment tools, in particular to help academic departments and colleges do program assessment for accreditation purposes. Others (see Cambridge, Cambridge, & Yancey, 2009) have focused more on supporting student learning by extending the portfolio's scope to include cocurricular and extracurricular experiences. A research team from George Mason University concludes: "Reflection doesn't happen in a vacuum; students need an audience and feedback in order for their e-portfolio practice to generate the results and habits of mind we wish to establish" (GMU, 2010). This orientation has led e-portfolio development to conceptually fit in with the new Web 2.0 media that open up new realms of collaboration beyond the campus. Students find new audiences with whom they collaborate and from whom they receive input to construct their understanding of course content well beyond the classroom boundaries. Models for these types of portfolios have been described in detail by John Zubizarreta (2004) and more recently by Cambridge, Cambridge, and Yancey (2009). These open learning portfolios provide instructors with a more comprehensive view of their students that includes aspects of their personal and professional lives, especially in the case of returning students. No other medium offers this opportunity as readily as an e-portfolio does.

Conclusion

This final chapter has made an argument for the usefulness of combining idea-based course design with hybrid or online learning. Increasingly, educators are predicting that in the near future, all college teaching will be "blended" or "hybrid" in nature. This chapter has demonstrated why that might be in the interest of both faculty and students. There are tangible advantages in using online technologies to help students work on authentic tasks, practice new skills step-by-step, receive ongoing feedback, learn how to assess their own progress, and always focus on the big picture to avoid losing themselves in an abundance of details. Guided by appropriate design, online technology can foster problem-based and self-directed learning in ways that the traditional face-to-face classroom cannot.

This does not happen automatically. Idea-based course design provides the pedagogical scaffold and the strategies for allowing technology-enhanced courses to support learning in novel ways. The key course design components outlined in this book determine where the capacities of online technology can be brought to bear. It is fortuitous that current online tools provide beneficial formats for having students discuss the essential questions underlying the core content, for mapping out its guiding concepts, and for confronting systematic barriers that get in the way of students' understanding. It is equally fortunate that the Web supports working on authentic performance tasks in unique ways, that key competencies can be practiced in unparalleled detail, and that the accomplishment of carefully derived learning outcomes can be reviewed and shared with various audiences in electronic portfolios that serve as assessment and learning tools at the same time. Idea-based course design and the online medium complement each other extremely well, but it is important to keep in mind that it is the course design that enables the learning and the online medium that accelerates it.

REFERENCES

Alliance for Excellent Education. (Sep. 2007). *Issue brief.* Washington, DC/: Author.

Amsel, E., Frost, R. B., & Johnston, A. (n.d.). *Misconceptions and conceptual change in undergraduate psychology students: The case of human uniqueness.* Retrieved April 19, 2009, from http://www.weber.edu/wsuimages/psychology/Docs/Assessment/ConceptualChange.pdf

Angelo, T. A., & Cross, K. P. (1993). *Classroom assessment techniques: A Handbook for college teachers* (2nd ed.). San Francisco, CA: Jossey-Bass.

Arter, J., & McTighe, J. (2001). *Scoring rubrics in the classroom: Using performance criteria for assessing and improvinig student performance.* Thousand Oaks, CA: Corwin Press.

Association of American Colleges and Universities (AAC&U). (2010). *Cognitive-structural measurements of personal and social responsibility development in students.* Retrieved February 26, 2010, from www.aacu.org/core_commitments/CognitiveStructuralMeasurements.cfm#LEP

Austhink. *Critical thinking on the Web.* Retrieved July 15, 2010, from www.austhink.org/critical/pages/definitions.html

Barke, H. D., Hazari, A., & Yitbarek, S. (2009). *Misconceptions in chemistry: Addressing perceptions in chemical education.* New York, NY: Springer.

Barkley, E. F. (2010). *Student engagement techniques: A handbook for college faculty.* San Francisco, CA: Jossey-Bass.

Barr, R. B., & Tagg, J. (1995). From teaching to learning: A new paradigm for undergraduate education. *Change, 27*(6), 12–25. Also at http://ilte.ius.edu/pdf/BarrTagg.pdf

Baxter-Magolda, M. (1987). *The affective dimension of learning: Student-faculty relationships that enhance intellectual development.* Oxford, OH: Miami University.

Belenky, M. F., Clinchy, B. M., Goldberger, N. R., & Tarule, J. M. (1986). *Women's ways of knowing: The development of self, voice, and mind.* New York, NY: Basic Books.

Bonk, C. J. (2009). *The world is open: How Web technology is revolutionizing education.* San Francisco, CA: Jossey-Bass.

Buckholdt, D. R., & Miller, G. E. (2009). Conclusion: Is stress likely to abate for faculty? In D. R. Buckholdt. & G. E. Miller (Eds.), *Faculty stress,* pp. 194–210. London: Routledge.

Cambridge, D., Cambridge, B., & Yancey, K. B. (Eds.). (2009). *Electronic portfolios 2.0: Emergent research on implementation and impact.* Sterling, VA: Stylus.

Center of Excellence in Leadership of Learning (CELL). (2009). *Summary of research on project-based learning.* Retrieved July 15, 2010, from http://cell.uindy.edu/docs/ PBL%20research%20summary.pdf

Davis, J. (2009). *Conceptual change: From emerging perspectives on learning, teaching and technology.* Retrieved June 1, 2011, from http://projects.coe.uga.edu/epltt/ index.php?title = Conceptual_Change

Dewey, J. (1938). *Experience and education.* New York, NY: Touchstone.

Donald, J. G. (2002). *Learning to think: Disciplinary perspectives.* San Francisco, CA: Jossey-Bass.

Donovan, M., & Bransford, J. (2005). *How students learn: History, mathematics, and science in the classroom.* Washington, DC: The National Academic Press.

Edutopia. (2001). *PBL research summary: Studies validate project-based learning.* Retrieved July 15, 2010, from http://www.edutopia.org/project-based-learning-research

Erickson, H. L. (2002). *Concept-based curriculum and instruction: Teaching beyond the facts.* Thousand Oaks, CA: Corwin Press.

Erickson, H. L. (2007). *Concept-based curriculum and instruction for the thinking classroom.* Thousand Oaks, CA: Corwin Press.

Fink, L. D. 2003. *Creating significant learning experiences: An integrated approach to designing college courses.* San Francisco: Jossey-Bass.

Gabriel, K. F. (2008). *Teaching unprepared students.* Sterling, VA: Stylus.

Gardner, H. (1991). *The unschooled mind: How children think and how schools should teach.* New York, NY: Basic Books.

George Mason University (GMU). (2010). *INCPR Final Report.* Retrieved February 20, 2010, from http://ncepr.org/finalreports/cohort3/George%20Mason%20 Final%20Report.pdf

Greene, J. P., & Winters, M. A. (2005, February). *Public high school graduation and college readiness rate: 1991–2002.* (Education Working Paper No. 8). New York, NY: Center for Civic Innovation at the Manhattan Institute for Policy Research.

Grunert O'Brien, J., Millis, B., Cohen, M., & Diamond, R. (2008). *The course syllabus: A learning-centered approach* (2nd ed.). San Francisco, CA: Jossey-Bass.

Harasim, L. (1990). *Online education: Perspectives on a new environment.* New York, NY: Praeger.

Haskell, R. E. (2000). *Transfer of learning: Cognition, instruction, and reasoning.* St. Louis, MO: Academic Press.

Higher Education Research Institute (HERI). (2008). *Faculty survey.* Los Angeles, CA: Graduate School of Education and Information Studies.

Huba, M. E., & Freed, J. E. (2000). *Learner-centered assessment on college campuses: Shifting the focus from teaching to learning.* Boston, MA: Allyn and Bacon.

Intel Teach Program. (2007). *Designing effective projects: Characteristics of projects. Benefits of project-based learning.* Retrieved July 15, 2010, from http://download .intel.com/education/Common/ph/Resources/DEP/projectdesign/DEP_pbl_re search.pdf

King, P. M., & Kitchener, K. S. (1994). *Developing reflective judgment.* San Francisco, CA: Jossey-Bass.

Kurfiss, J. G. (1988). *Critical thinking: Theory, research, practice, and possibilities.* Washington, DC: Association for the Study of Higher Education.

Kujawski, T. A., & Kowalski, P. (2004). Naive psychological science: The prevalence, strength, and sources of misconceptions. *The Psychological Record, 54*(1), 15–25.

Lang, J. M. (2005). *Life on the tenure track: Lessons from the first year.* Baltimore, MD: The Johns Hopkins University Press.

Library of Congress. (2000). "Constructing history: How historians see the light." *The learning page.* Retrieved June 1, 2011, from www.coe.uga.edu/epltt/cc_example/module1/source.html

Lilienfeld, S., Lynn, S., Ruscio, J., & Beyerstein, B. (2009). *50 Great myths of popular psychology: Shattering widespread misconceptions about human behavior.* Hoboken, NJ: Wiley-Blackwell.

McTighe, J., & Wiggins, G. (2004). *Understanding by design: Professional development workbook.* Alexandria, VA: Association for Supervision and Curriculum Development.

Menges, R. J. (1996). Experiences of new hired faculty. In L. Richlin (Ed.), *To improve the academy, 15,* (169–182). Stillwater, OK: New Forums Press.

Mestre, J. P. (2005). *Transfer of learning: Research and perspectives.* Charlotte, NC: Information Age Publishing.

Missouri Department of Elementary and Secondary Education. (2005). *Misconceptions in science.* Retrieved April 19, 2009, from http//dese.mo.gov/divimprove/curriculum/science/SciMisconc11.05.pdf

Mitchell, R. (1992). *Testing for learning: How new approaches to evaluation can improve American schools.* New York, NY: The Free Press.

Moon, J. (2007). *Critical thinking: An exploration of theory and practice.* New York, NY: Routledge.

National Center for Education Statistics. (2006). *Digest of Education Statistics 2005.* Washington, DC: U.S. Department of Education.

New York Science Teacher. (n.d.). *Science misconceptions.* Retrieved April 19, 2009, from http//www.newyorkscienceteacher.com/sci/miscon/index.php

Nilson, L. B. (2007). *The graphic syllabus and the outcomes map: Communicating your course.* San Francisco, CA: Jossey-Bass.

Novak, J. D., & Cañas, A. J. (2006). *The theory underlying concept maps and how to construct them.* Retrieved June 1, 2011, from http://cmap.ihmc.us/publications/researchpapers/theorycmaps/theoryunderlyingconceptmaps.htm

Palloff, R. M., & Pratt, K. (2005). *Collaborating online: Learning together in community.* San Francisco, CA: Jossey-Bass.

Palloff, R. M., & Pratt, K. (2007). *Building online learning communities: Effective strategies for the virtual classroom.* San Francisco, CA: Jossey-Bass.

Paul, R., & Elder, L. (2001). *Critical thinking: Tools for taking charge of your learning and your life.* Upper Saddle River, NJ: Prentice Hall.

Penn State University (PSU). (2009). *INCPR Final Report.* Retrieved February 20, 2010, from http://ncepr.org/finalreports/cohort3/Penn%20State%20Final%20 Report.pdf

Perry, W. G. (1970). *Forms of intellectual and ethical development in the college years: A scheme.* Troy, MO: Holt, Rinehart & Winston.

Problem-Based Learning Clearinghouse. University of Delaware. Retrieved February 4, 2010, from https://primus.nss.udel.edu/Pbl/

Rhem, J. (1995). Deep/surface approaches to learning: An introduction. *The National Teaching and Learning Forum, 5,* 1–5.

Rose, C., Minton, L., & Arline, C. (2006). *Uncovering student thinking in mathematics: 25 formative assessment probes.* Thousand Oaks, CA: Corwin Press.

Ruscio, J. (2005). *Critical thinking in psychology: Separating sense from nonsense.* Florence, KY: Wadsworth.

Saljo, R. (1979). Learning in the learner's perspective. I. Some common-sense conceptions. *Reports from the Institute of Education, University of Gotheborg, 76. ERIC Document 173369*

Stenstrom, D., & Iyer, R. (2010). PsychWiki. Retrieved February 10, 2010, from www.psychwiki.com

Stepans, J. (2003). *Targeting students' science misconceptions: Physical science concepts using the conceptual change model.* Riverview, FL: Idea Factory.

Stevens, D. D., & Levi, A. J. (2005). *Introduction to rubrics: An assessment tool to save grading time, convey effective feedback and promote student learning.* Sterling, VA: Stylus.

Stiehl, R., & Lewchuk, L. (2002). *The outcomes primer: Reconstructing the college curriculum* (2nd ed.). Corvallis, OR: The Learning Organization.

Stiehl, R., & Lewchuk, L. (2005). *The mapping primer: Tools for reconstructing the college curriculum.* Corvallis, OR: The Learning Organization.

Stiehl, R., & Lewchuk, L. (2008). *The assessment primer: Creating a flow of learning evidence.* Corvallis, OR: The Learning Organization.

Stigler, J., & Hiebert, J. (1997). Understanding and improving classroom mathematics instruction: An overview of the TIMSS video study. *Phi Delta Kappan, 79*(1), 14–21.

Suskie, L. (2004). *Assessing student learning: A common sense guide.* Bolton, MA: Anker.

Taylor, K., Marienau, C., & Fiddler, M. (2000). *Developing adult learners: Strategies for teachers and trainers.* San Francisco: Jossey-Bass.

Tewksbury, B. J., & Macdonald, R. H. (2005). *On the cutting edge—Professional development for geoscience faculty: Designing effective and innovative courses.* Retrieved May 1, 2009, from http://serc.carleton.edu/NAGTWorkshops/course design/index.html

Thomas, J. W. (2000). *A review of research on project-based learning.* Retrieved July 15, 2010, from http://www.bobpearlman.org/BestPractices/PBL_Research.pdf

Tomlinson, C. A., Kaplan, S. N., Renzulli, J. S., Purcell, J., Leppien, J., & Burns, D. (2002). *The parallel curriculum: A design to develop high potential and challenge high-ability learners.* Thousand Oaks, CA: Corwin Press.

Tyler, R. W. (1949). *Basic principles of curriculum and instruction.* Chicago, IL: The University of Chicago Press.

Walvoord, B. E., & Anderson, V. J. (1998). *Effective grading: A tool for learning and assessment.* San Francisco, CA: Jossey-Bass.

Weigel, V. B. (2002). *Deep learning for a digital age: Technology's untapped potential to enrich higher education.* San Francisco, CA: Jossey-Bass.

Wiggins, G. (1998). *Educative assessment: Designing assessments to inform and improve student performance.* San Francisco, CA: Jossey-Bass.

Wiggins, G., & McTighe, J. (2005). *Understanding by design* (2nd ed.). Alexandria, VA: Association for Supervision and Curriculum Development.

Ziegenfuss, D. H. (2007a). A phenomenographic analysis of course design in the academy. *Journal of Ethnographic and Qualitative Research, 2,* 70–79.

Ziegenfuss, D. H. (2007b). Refocusing the lens: The priority of understanding course design approaches. *POD Annual Conference, October 25–28, 2007* (pp. 1–6). Pittsburgh, PA.

Zubizarreta, J. (2004). *The learning portfolio: Reflective practice for improving student learning.* San Francisco, CA: Jossey-Bass (Anker).

PY-624: THEORIES OF MOTIVATION

A course for seniors and graduate students

SYLLABUS

TABLE OF CONTENTS

The Purpose of This Course

We all make assumptions about what it takes to influence others in a positive manner. In this course, we will probe some of these assumptions about why people do the things they do. We will look at the values we are embracing by defining mental health with characteristics such as self-esteem, achievement motivation, intrinsic actions, caring families, self-restraint, or positive thinking. Because most of you will be going into the "helping professions," you need to know what it takes to help other people make significant changes in their lives. But you can't change others without first experiencing intentional change in

(NOTE: Course policies and other minor details usually addressed in a syllabus are left out here.)

your own life. Therefore, this course wants to help you gain some clarity about the motivational principles that help you take charge of your life.

Let's start with the big picture. Every discipline is based on some "big ideas" that guide the assumptions researchers make and, thereby, ultimately the findings they come up with. The big ideas that are most relevant for this course include the following.

Big Idea 1: Causes of Behavior

We all tend to believe that each behavior has a specific cause and that, if we find that cause, we can change the behavior. The question is: Is that true and, if yes, are there different types of causes for different types of behavior?

Big Idea 2: Individual Differences

All of us recognize from time to time that different people seem to function differently. We see behaviors that seem influenced by personality differences, gender differences, age differences, educational differences, cultural, ethnic, and even national differences. Are there any discernable factors that underlie all these differences?

Big Idea 3: Psychological Theorizing

We have come to realize that different scientific fields use different approaches to generate knowledge. Among those differences are the kinds of theories that sciences create. Which types of theories do psychologists develop, and have they always developed their theories in the same way?

Big Idea 4: Qualitative Research

Learning how people function requires some observational tools. These tools can involve the experimental setup of a controlled, artificial scenario in which people have a limited range of options on how to behave, or they can involve fairly open-ended forms of interviews and observation that allow respondents to react in unforeseen ways. Qualitative research claims that the latter are the preferred tools for understanding human behavior at a deeper level.

Map of Big Ideas, Enduring Understandings, and Learning Outcomes

The big ideas are only the first broad outline of what we want to accomplish by the end of this course. The "concept map" shows you in more detail what the course is about. You will see three layers of increasingly more specific goals for the course: (1) The Big Ideas, (2) Enduring Understandings that are derived from the ideas, and (3) Learning Outcomes that are derived from the Enduring Understandings.

The Biweekly Course Cycle

Our textbook *Understanding Motivation and Emotion*, like other textbooks on this topic, is divided into parts that address different aspects of motivation and emotion, including needs, cognition, individual differences, and emotions. Within those parts, different chapters discuss key theories and concepts that are relevant to each main topic. Instead of strictly following this structure, I have decided to divide the course into what you might call different "domains" of motivation. We will address six of them:

- **Self-Concept:** the motivation to develop a positive sense of identity
- **Attachment:** the motivation to belong to a social unit for emotional security
- **Curiosity:** the motivation to learn and explore new things
- **Achievement:** the motivation to succeed in the goals you set for yourself
- **Ego Defenses:** the tendency to develop attitudes that preserve a positive sense of self
- **Arousal:** the biological mechanisms that raise people's desire for action

This allows us to divide most of the semester into two-week modules, one for each of the six motivation domains. Within each of these two-week modules, you can expect to encounter the following activities:

- An introduction of the motivation domain with a short video that demonstrates a real-life application
- Short lecture vignettes on the theoretical framework for the current content block, followed by various classroom activities
- Group-work discussing the progress on the individual research projects, including problems encountered or anticipated
- Short lecture vignettes on the qualitative research process or on psychological theorizing
- Module-quiz and practice opportunities for essential competencies regarding course content and the research project

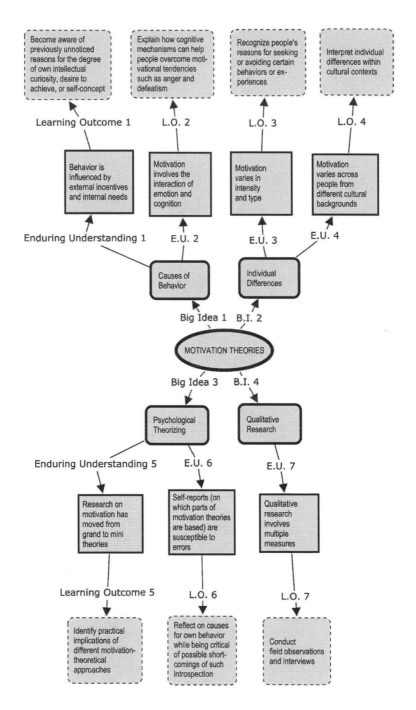

Course Requirements

Main Reading

Reeve, J. (2008). *Understanding Motivation and Emotion* (5th ed.). Hoboken, NJ: Wiley Publishers.

Main Project

This course wants to help you learn motivation theories in the context of real-world applications that are similar to the ones you would encounter in your future as a professional psychologist. You will spend time outside of the classroom doing some research, for which a variety of course activities will prepare you. You have several options for your research project, the details of which are explained on the next page.

Module Quizzes

Each of the six two-week modules on the different domains of motivation will end in a quiz with mostly multiple-choice questions about key concepts and theories of the motivation domain as well as questions about research procedures discussed during the past two weeks. Your lowest quiz performance will be dropped. Each quiz will also serve as another opportunity to review pertinent course material before we move to the next module.

Short Reflections About the Course

It is important that you understand the framework and intended learning outcomes for this course. To help with that, you will do three short reflections that use the course description in this syllabus.

The *first* reflection (Week 1) uses the elaboration on the Big Ideas (Syllabus, pp. 1–2) in conjunction with the concept map that links Big Ideas to Enduring Understandings and Learning Outcomes (Syllabus, p. 3). At this early point in the course, it is okay if you do not fully understand how it all fits together, but you should begin making some connections and raising questions about the things that you don't understand yet. The ability to raise questions is critical for this course.

The *second* reflection (Week 5) asks you to connect the Course Learning Outcomes with the main course project. As you observe and interview the respondents in your project, what questions should you have on your mind that would address the concerns in (maybe not all, but most of) the course learning outcomes? For example, regarding learning outcome #4 ("Interpret individual differences within cultural contexts"), you might look for retirement community residents from different cultural backgrounds and explore how their satisfaction with their current living arrangements might be connected to the differences in their cultural background, such as education level, social class/status, ethnicity, and so on. Keep in mind, though, that the questions you have as a researcher are usually not identical to the interview questions you actually ask.

The *third* reflection (Week 15) requires you to consider the whole conceptual framework for the course. Now that you understand all the concepts, you should look for ideas in the course that are related to ideas from other courses (in and outside the program). Psychology, like any other science, does not consist of totally self-contained subfields. Motivation theories play a role in social psychology, developmental psychology, I/O psychology, clinical psychology, and so on. They also play a role in sociology, education, political science, business, and many more. Which of the concepts and theories we discussed in this course seem particularly relevant to you for other fields? Provide examples.

Rubrics Development

The syllabus contains performance criteria for each of the five parts of the main course project (see pp. 4–5). As a collaborative activity, we will spend some time in mid-semester to develop more detailed rubrics for part 4 (Data Analysis) and part 5 (Oral Presentation) of the course project. This will not be a graded activity, but it determines how the key parts of your project will be assessed.

Grading of Student Performance

	Grade Percentages
6 Module Quizzes (lowest-scoring quiz is dropped) (5% each)	25%
3 Short Reflection Papers (3%, 3%, and 4%)	10%
Course Project:	
1. Identify issue and target population	05%
2. Create research design	10%
3. Collect data	15%
4. Analyze data	20%
5. Present findings	15%
TOTAL	100%

Main Course Project

The Authentic Performance Task

The following is a detailed description of the main assignment for this course. It involves a research project that unfolds in several phases over 10 weeks of the semester. You have several options to choose from and can even come up with your own project, as long as I approve it. The next paragraphs describe the general format and procedure for this assignment, no matter which specific project you choose.

CONTEXT: We have an aging population in the United States, with large proportions of people living decades past retirement age. Many of them find themselves in various types of retirement homes or communities. Many retirees seem to enjoy the relatively carefree state this stage of their lives provides; others feel bored and increasingly isolated from the rest of society. Issues such as changing self-concept, decreasing family ties, lack of challenge and opportunities for achievement, pessimism, and other aspects of motivation and emotion come into play in this environment. What can be done to keep the members of such retirement communities engaged and meaningfully challenged?

ROLE: You are a gerontologist who has been hired as a consultant by the director of the _____ retirement community to look into the mental health of the members of this community. You are given 10 weeks to complete your investigation and deliver your report.

TASK: You start by getting a general impression of the community. That implies questions such as: Which activities do the retirees engage in? Which seniors seem happier than others? What factors seem to play a major role in these discrepancies? You also want to talk with a few carefully selected members of the community and conduct interviews with both the seniors and staff. These interviews should gently probe into some of the issues mentioned under "context." The analysis of your observations and interviews should result in concrete recommendations about what works well in the community and what aspects of community life might need improvement.

PRODUCT: Your final report is to be given in two formats: (1) a paper that is handed in to your instructor for review and (2) a 10-minute presentation to the director (or other management staff) of the retirement community. The presentation can be either given in class with the director present or via live or recorded video presented to the director.

ASSESSOR: Although the course instructor is the main assessor of the project, who will ultimately assign a final grade (based on the attached grading rubric), the director of the retirement community will also provide feedback to you either orally or in writing. That feedback will indicate the practical usefulness of your report and the likelihood that any of the recommendations might be implemented in the future.

Below find three additional options for a similar task from a different context. If you have a preference for another context, to which you have access, talk to me.

- You are a school psychologist who has been asked to investigate the trials and tribulations of being a senior at _____ High School. Your report should include observations regarding questions such as: Is the senior year in high school a lost time for education? Are students still intellectually engaged and challenged? You should include recommendations for improvement.
- You are a sports psychologist working with the local _____ team. The team has gone through some rough times lately and needs some insight into what has gone wrong and what can be done to motivate players (and staff) to turn things around.
- You are an industrial and organizational psychologist who has been called upon to consult on the dwindling numbers of volunteer workers in a local charitable organization. Your task is to find out what motivates the current volunteers to donate their time to the organization, as well as what turns them off. Your insight and recommendations are to be used to give more compelling arguments in the organization's recruitment efforts.

[Here is Plan-B with a performance task that is less authentic but could substitute for the above options, if necessary:

If the logistical arrangements for the above tasks seem too difficult to manage, they could be modified by providing students with cases from the literature (or having students find their own cases) that provide most of the required context. Students may then simply do interviews with a few representatives of the target group, whom they know or can reach without having to obtain institutional consent. Together with the literature/cases, those interviews would then provide the basis for the students' reports.]

Criteria for Grading your Project

Performance Criteria for Task

Your project is divided into five parts that are due at different times of the semester. Each part is graded separately. Below find three to four criteria that I will consider in grading each part. These criteria are not just meant for grading purposes, but also to provide guidance for your work. Each criterion is elaborated on with a couple of questions that you should ask yourself as you work on this part of the project. We will also take class time to discuss the various criteria, create rubrics for parts 4 and 5, and practice the skills and competencies you need to live up to these criteria in your own project.

PART 1: Identify issue and target population

Explain reason for choosing main issue and target population.
- Why did you choose the gerontology vs. school psych vs. sports psych vs. I/O psych issue?
- Any personal link to the target population?

Identify related motivation-theoretical concepts.
- Which of the six "types" of motivation are involved?
- Which key concepts do you expect to include?

Consider problems with access.
- Which access problems would you anticipate?
- Any strategies or personal connections for obtaining access?

PART 2: Create an effective research design (with logistics)

Explain how to get access to respondents.
- How do you intend to establish trust with the administration?
- How do you intend to establish trust with the seniors?

Establish workable observation and interview schedule.
- What is your plan week-by-week that allows you to finish the project in 10 weeks?
- Which respondents do you intend to interview? Why them, and when are they available?

Review relevant literature to provide focus for observation and interviews.
- What does the literature say about the living conditions and dynamics in retirement communities?
- What does the literature say about new trends in retirement life?

Create interview guide.
- What do you want to ask?
- How and in what sequence should you ask it?

PART 3: Collect data

Implement observation and interview schedule.
- Did you have enough time for your observation/interview task?
- Did you prepare yourself and your respondents ahead of time?

Take proper field notes.
- How should you organize your field notes?
- What's important to write down?

Separate field notes from subjective reflections.
- What was actually said, seen, or done by those you observed or interviewed?
- What were your additional impressions and reflections about it?

PART 4: Analyze data

Categorize data into appropriate clusters.
- What themes are you pursuing, or what themes are emerging from your work?
- How do those themes (clusters of data) connect with each other?

Connect observations with appropriate theoretical concepts.
- Which observations seem to fit with which theoretical concepts?
- Which essential questions does your research project help you answer?
- Are there observations that seem to contradict certain theoretical concepts?

Identify social and personal implications.
- What do your observations say about the mental health of those seniors?
- Did you derive any personal insights from those observations?

Reflect on potential shortcomings.
- What would you do differently if you were to repeat this mini-study?
- Which aspects of your research did you find most problematic?

PART 5: Present findings

Be clear and concise.
- What are the main points that you need to explain about your research?
- How can you present them properly in 10 minutes?

Explain data collection and analysis.
- What do you need to present about your data collection process?
- What were the key insights from your study?

Provide logical and pertinent recommendations.
- Which changes would you recommend?

With what caveats do your recommendations come?

Course Outline

Week	Essential Questions	Assignments
1	Introduction	Reflection on big ideas, enduring understandings, and learning outcomes
2	Self-Concept: How can self-esteem be changed?	
	Self-Concept: Can emotions (e.g., anger) be controlled by cognitions? How does what we think influence what we feel?	
3	Course: How do the different elements of this course fit together?	
	Methodology: What motivates you, and how is that similar or different from what motivates others?	QUIZ 1
4	Attachment: Does single-parenthood lead to mal-adjustment in children?	Project, Part 1: Identify appropriate issue and target population
	Attachment: Are attachment patterns different across cultures?	
5	Methodology: Can we directly observe the causes of our actions?	Reflection on how the authentic performance task addresses (which) learning outcomes
	Methodology: How do observers in the field establish trust with those they observe?	QUIZ 2
6	Curiosity: Why are so many young people "bored" with their jobs/school/life?	
	Curiosity: How can rewards undermine motivation?	
7	Methodology: How can you tell whether interviewees tell the truth?	Project, Part 2: Create an effective research design (with logistics)
	Methodology: How does the question format influence the information value of the response?	QUIZ 3

8	Achievement: Why do people in some cultures develop a higher need for achievement than people in other cultures?	
	Achievement: Is goal-setting enough to increase achievement?	
9	Theories: Do multiple "mini-theories" explain human behavior better than comprehensive attempts at theory-building?	
	Theories: What is the difference between a motivational principle and a motivational theory?	QUIZ 4
10	Ego Defenses: Why do different people develop different explanations (optimism/pessimism) for what happens to them?	
	Ego Defenses: Do we need to create a false sense of reality to maintain our "sanity"?	
11	Methodology: Where are introspections deceiving (see Attribution Theory)?	Project, Part 3: Collect data
	Methodology: How generalizable are data from one context to another?	QUIZ 5
12	Arousal: Which experiences are "stressful"?	
	Arousal: Is risk-taking necessary for feeling alive?	
13	Course: How is motivation linked with the rest of psychology?	Project, Part 4: Analyze data
		QUIZ 6
14	Student presentations	Project, Part 5: Present findings
	Student presentations	
15	Student presentations	
	Student presentations	Reflection on how concepts/ ideas from this course relate to other courses
16	Discussion on links of course concepts with other courses	

Note: To keep this overview readable, reading assignments are not included in this table.

Also available from Stylus

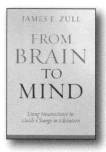

From Brain to Mind
Using Neuroscience as a Guide for Change in Education
James E. Zull

With his knack for making science intelligible for the layman, and his ability to illuminate scientific concepts through analogy and reference to personal experience, James Zull—the acclaimed author of *The Art of Changing the Brain*—offers the reader an engrossing and coherent introduction to what neuroscience can tell us about cognitive development through experience, and its implications for education.

Stating that the time is ripe to recognize that "the primary objective of education is to understand human learning" and that "all other objectives depend on achieving this understanding", James Zull challenges readers to focus on this purpose, first for themselves, and then for those for whose learning they are responsible.

The New Digital Shoreline
How Web 2.0 and Millennials Are Revolutionizing Higher Education
Roger McHaney

"A masterly and authoritative presentation of the topography of the new digital shoreline that will be invaluable to his fellow faculty."—*Sir John Daniel, President, Commonwealth of Learning, and former Vice-Chancellor of The Open University*

Two seismic forces beyond our control—the advent of Web 2.0 and the inexorable influx of tech-savvy Millennials on campus—are shaping what Roger McHaney calls "The New Digital Shoreline" of higher education. Failure to chart its contours, and adapt, poses a major threat to higher education as we know it.

These forces demand that we as educators reconsider the learning theories, pedagogies, and practices on which we have depended, and modify our interactions with students and peers—all without sacrificing good teaching, or lowering standards, to improve student outcomes.

This book argues for nothing less than a reinvention of higher education to meet these new realities. Just adding technology to our teaching practices will not suffice. McHaney calls for a complete rethinking of our practice of teaching to meet the needs of this emerging world and envisioning ourselves as connected, co-learners with our students.

Team-Based Learning in the Social Sciences and Humanities
Group Work that Works to Generate Critical Thinking and Engagement
Edited by Michael Sweet and Larry K. Michaelsen

Team-Based Learning (TBL) is a unique, powerful, and proven form of small-group learning that is being increasingly adopted in higher education. Teachers who use TBL report high levels of engagement, critical thinking, and retention among their students. TBL has been used successfully in both small and large classes, in computer-supported and online classes; and because it is group work that works, it has been implemented in nearly every discipline and in several countries around the world.

This book introduces the elements of TBL and how to apply them in the social sciences and humanities. It describes the four essential elements of TBL—readiness assurance, design of application exercises, permanent teams, peer evaluation—and pays particular attention to the specification of learning outcomes, which can be a unique challenge in these fields.

Sty/us

22883 Quicksilver Drive
Sterling, VA 20166-2102

Subscribe to our e-mail alerts: www.Styluspub.com